Growir

C000246632

Flora Winfield is an Anglican priest, and is Local Unity Secretary for the Church of England's Council for Christian Unity. She has worked in Local Ecumenical Partnerships, as a County Ecumenical Officer and as Chaplain to Mansfield College, Oxford, a college of URC tradition. She wrote *Travelling Together* (CTE Publications, 1995) with Elizabeth Welch and is the author of *Releasing Energy* (Church House Publishing, 2000).

Growing Together
Working for Unity Locally

FLORA WINFIELD

Published in Great Britain in 2002 by
Society for Promoting Christian Knowledge
Holy Trinity Church
Marylebone Road
London NW1 4DU

British Library Cataloguing-in-Publication Data
A catalogue record for this book is available from the
British Library

ISBN 0-281-05348-0

Typeset by Pioneer Associates, Perthshire
Printed in Great Britain by
Antony Rowe, Chippenham, Wiltshire

Contents

Foreword

Flora Winfield is honest enough to recognize that, in large part, the reality of people's ecumenical experience has been less than exhilarating. For many – if not for most – it has proved a poor anaemic thing; consisting largely in a repetitive (and, frankly, boring) cycle of 'activities' – in which 'washing up in other people's church kitchens' always seems to feature somewhere along the line!

She points us towards a clearer understanding and a better way. Reminding us that, although we must beware of defining each other *solely* in terms of that which differentiates us, neither must we disparage those differences; for they represent the authentic expression of the journeys that have brought our several traditions to where they are today. 'Unity is not uniformity' – and true unity resides not in the elimination of the distinctive, but in learning to understand and value it. As specificity is the God-given key to a created order that modern physics tells us is *necessarily* diverse, so the differences between our Christian traditions, far from presenting a threat, offer real opportunities for mutual growth and enrichment.

It is hardly surprising, then, that the bland and unexceptionable sort of ecumenical activity that fears to deal in the currency of difference has warmed few hearts in the Church and cut little ice in the world.

But if unity is not about uniformity, then it is most certainly about friendship; and especially about the honesty and give and take of friendship. The friendship that takes pleasure in the other's strengths and skills, that is content to respect when it cannot understand and that remains ready to love even when it finds that liking is difficult.

In all sorts of ways, this is an essentially *practical* book. It offers a helpful series of sketches of our sister churches as seen 'from the inside'. It shows just how much can be done, and is being done within a framework of canon law that is actually far more supportive than it is restrictive of ecumenical endeavour. But perhaps most helpfully of all, Flora Winfield has clothed her discourse with accounts of the hands-on experience of those who, in every corner of our land, have accepted the risks and won the rewards of real-time ecumenical encounter.

In an age when the general appetite for ecumenism seems sadly jaded, this timely contribution offers both a challenge to the indifferent and valuable resources to the ready.

✠ David Ebor:

Preface: What Kind of Unity Are We Working for?

FRIENDSHIP

The best work for unity is always about friendship; whether in practical witness and service to local communities or around the table in theological dialogues, it is often friendship that keeps us together when things are difficult, and it is through coming to know one another and working together that we also come to recognize in one another's traditions the common faith that we share. There is no substitute for this growing into unity in relationship with one another; and it is as we grow in our friendship that we come not only to recognize the faith that we hold in common, but also to value the diversity of our traditions, which express the good news through different cultures and temperaments, shaped by different historical experience and context, and that emphasize different aspects of the gospel.

THE CHURCH AS FOOD FOR A HUNGRY WORLD

As we grow in our friendship for one another through our work together, our divisions seem increasingly cruel and ridiculous; they impede our sharing in God's mission to a broken and divided world, and they fracture and distort our proclamation of the gospel of healing and liberation. God offers his Church as food for a hungry world, setting before the needy and the broken a feast; but we are constantly trying to serve this feast from broken tables, each tradition impoverished by our division and all of us lacking integrity and credibility because of it. It is my experience that, in order to keep finding the energy to work for unity, you need not only a rich, Spirit-filled vision of Christ's body united, but also a sense of anger, of offence about the churches' dividedness.

DIVERSITY AND DIVIDEDNESS

None of this is to deny that there are real differences between us: differences that go beyond diversity and into contradiction and conflict. But these differences will never be healed either by our ignoring one another or by our ignoring the things that really divide us. We cannot live complacently with a broken Church, but neither will we participate in its healing by pretending that we are really all the same. We are not all the same, but it is not our diversity that is the problem, but our division along lines not only of doctrine and ecclesiology, but of race, class, ethnicity and culture. The idea that in order to be united we must become uniform is one of the greatest difficulties to overcome in working for unity. Each of our traditions reflects different aspects of the gospel; each of us has guarded, during our years of division, gifts of the Spirit to the Church which are part of our common Christian heritage. We do not grow into unity by becoming more blandly like one another, but by learning afresh the value and beauty of our own tradition, encountered in new ways as it is shared with others.

Each of us has what the others lack.

SO WHY WORK FOR UNITY?

Work for unity is important because the Church is important; as we proclaim the good news of the word made flesh we do so not only in words but in the way we live as communities in relationship with one another and with God. Think about these questions: What could someone from beyond the Christian community learn about the gospel by studying the churches in your local area? Not just what they say but what they are? How do they relate to one another and to the rest of the community? As we relate to one another in all our diversity, we can offer a pattern for living joyfully with difference, and also begin to reflect something of God's own life, in the Trinity of Persons in community.

There are plenty of good reasons to work for unity: it makes us more effective, more efficient, more credible, more coherent; but ultimately there is only one really important reason – the brokenness of the Church is offensive, it grieves God's heart. And our unity is his will, his longing desire.

So I hope that you will find in this book some fresh inspiration to become involved in or renew your commitment to working for unity, and some new ways of asking the question: What kind of unity would speak to the world about this kind of God?

Flora Winfield
Portadown, Co. Armagh
August 2000

Introduction

WHY I WANTED TO WRITE THIS BOOK

As Local Unity Secretary for the Church of England's Council for
Christian Unity, I have spent much of the past five years visiting
churches around England, meeting people who are working for
unity, or who would like to. Many of these people share a sense of
impatience and shame about the disunity of the Church, and also a
longing to work together more effectively and credibly in mission,
and in the service of their local community. So much progress
towards the reconciliation of different Christian traditions has been
made over the last century. There is a great deal to celebrate, as
Christians in many different contexts have experienced afresh the
call to receive together the gift of unity, often in response to the
missionary imperative, to persecution or to the need to witness
together against political injustice or great social evils. Partly in
response to the great upheavals of the twentieth century, churches
have been drawn to take counsel together, and institutions that enable
this have come in to being. The World Council of Churches, the Conference of European Churches and the British Council of Churches
all grew out of the turmoil of two world wars and their politically
divided aftermath. But this response to God's call to unity has also
arisen out of a sense of the sinfulness of the churches' divisions,
especially in the context of mission, and a renewed understanding of
the importance of the theology of the Trinity in showing us what it
means to be in relationship to one another and to God.

In England, there are many places where Christians have grown
together in friendship and understanding as well as in faith, life and
witness over the past fifty years; there are no magic formulas for
making this happen, but there are plenty of good ideas, and I want
to share some of them, so that others can benefit from this experience and so can be renewed and encouraged in working for unity.

In my travels, I have also met quite a few people who were per-
plexed or downhearted about the progress of work for unity, and I

hope that this book might offer some theological help as well as practical encouragement.

My own work for unity is rooted in personal experience in ministry, in Gloucester, Milton Keynes, Oxford and London. I have often struggled with this work, and sometimes become discouraged at the pace of development; but we have come a long way in the last fifty years, since a time when we often could not worship, work or pray together and, indeed, behaved as if we were in competition with one another. There is a great deal to be thankful for, even if the common task of bringing the good news of healing and liberation to a broken and divided world keeps us impatient for that unity which is both God's gift to us and our calling.

WHO IS THIS BOOK INTENDED FOR?

If you are already involved in working for unity, I hope that this book will provide a useful source; a place where you can look up ideas, develop and renew your own reasons for involvement and find some fresh resources.

If you would like to become involved in working for unity, this book offers some of the background to how we have got to where we are and outlines the imperatives for working for unity and some of the ways of going about it. *Growing Together* focuses on ecumenical work in England, seen from a Church of England perspective, but I hope that those from other traditions will also find it a useful resource.

Growing Together is in seven sections. The Preface examines some of the reasons for working for unity. The Introduction looks at why I put this book together and explains how it can be used. It also includes preliminary exercises on first reactions to the word 'ecumenism' and on the motivations for working for unity.

The first chapter, 'Why Does Division Matter?' takes an honest look at some of the existing work for unity, and at the ways in which the dividedness of the Church is perceived. It sets the whole ecumenical task in the context of a divided world, and looks at examples from Northern Ireland and the Balkans. It goes on to examine questions of identity and belonging, and there are exercises to help you look at the divisions within your own community, and to enable those who want to develop honesty in their ecumenical relationships to share the spiritual treasures of their traditions.

In Chapter 2, 'Who Are Your Partner Churches?' those from

partner churches and groups of churches in England set out a brief description of their church or family of churches, its ethos, character and spiritual tradition. They describe the kinds of church structure and ministry you might encounter. Some sources for further information about the churches are included at the end of the book in 'Useful Sources of Information'. There are exercises to look at the different ways in which people become part of a particular church, and at who the partner churches are in your own community. This section also includes information on Churches Together in England and Churches Together in Britain and Ireland.

Chapter 3, 'Are We Really Allowed to do This?' sets out the framework for working for unity provided by the possibilities for sharing ministry and worship permitted by the Church of England Ecumenical Canons, B43 and B44, and offers a range of examples of how these canons may be used.

Chapter 4, 'What Does It Mean to be the People of God in This Place?' begins with an exploration of different understandings of 'local' and after an exercise on looking at your own locality then offers examples of various ways of working together in different kinds of communities – rural areas, market towns, inner cities, housing estates, suburbs and new housing areas. The emphasis is on understanding locality and responding to the needs of the human community in witness and service.

Finally, Chapter 5, 'Is It Worth All the Effort?' looks at some of the dynamics at work in ecumenical relationships; here you will find theological reflection on relationships and community, and on the process of moving through repentance, reconciliation, renewal and *kenosis*, self-emptying, towards *koinonia*, communion with God and with one another in and through God. The exercises are based around the planning of an away day or weekend either as a parish or deanery or with partner churches, and are aimed to break down stereotypes and to name fears and difficulties in a positive atmosphere, leading to renewed relationships and fresh approaches to witness and service.

WAYS OF USING THIS BOOK

Growing Together can be used as a reference book, and as a source book for ideas; it is also structured with questions for reflection and discussion and exercises to share with groups or work through on your own. The sections could be used to resource sessions for house groups or provide material for a parish, deanery or Churches Together away day or weekend.

BEFORE WE BEGIN ...

For those who have already glimpsed the ecumenical vision, it can be hard to understand that ecumenism might not be a word with completely positive associations for everyone. For most of us, the experience of ecumenism will be a mixed one – just as most of our experience of our church, relationships and life are mixed. But the imperative to unity remains just as strong, however imperfect its expression in local contexts.

- What is your experience of working for unity?
- What does the word 'ecumenism' mean for you?

I have asked these questions of many groups of Christians over the last few years; here are a few of the responses which arise almost every time people answer truthfully:

- boring Lent groups
- dull and characterless worship
- lots of extra meetings
- an optional extra
- an enthusiasm from the 1960s and 1970s
- a distraction from the proper task, which is mission/evange-lism/turning the world upside down/doing really perfect BCP matins/whatever
- an excuse to do whatever you like, regardless of your church's tradition, theology, rules and discipline
- John 17
- papering over the cracks
- compromise, a sell-out
- being obsessed with structures
- more meetings
- taking adventures in mission together
- a gospel imperative
- the longing for unity
- discovering different ways of worshipping and praying and enjoying it
- something for young people

- something for a previous generation
- something for other people
- a round of activities which we are made to feel guilty about if we don't support them
- a response to a broken world
- small churches being taken over by large, powerful, rich churches
- large churches being taken over by small, articulate, confident churches
- working for peace and world development
- discovering fellowship
- discovering your own tradition by sharing it
- Christian Aid week
- something the vicar is keen on
- some of the congregation are keen on it
- washing up in other people's church kitchens.

Whatever your experience of ecumenism, I hope that *Growing Together* will enable you to take some new steps with your partner churches, and that it will lead you too to conclude that ecumenism is far too important to be left to ecumenists.

Abbreviations and Other Terms

ACTS   Action of Churches Together in Scotland
ARC   Anglican–Roman Catholic Committee
ARCIC   Anglican–Roman Catholic International Commission
BCC   British Council of Churches
BCP   Book of Common Prayer
BEC   British Evangelical Council
BWA   Baptist World Alliance
CCBI   Council of Churches for Britain and Ireland
CEC   Conference of European Churches
CEOs   county ecumenical officers
CTBI   Churches Together in Britain and Ireland
CTE   Churches Together in England
CWM   Council for World Mission
Cytun   Churches Together in Wales
DEOs   denominational ecumenical officers
EA   Evangelical Alliance
Enfys   Covenant for Union in Wales
FCC   Free Churches Council
LEPs   Local Ecumenical Partnerships
PCCs   parochial church councils
URC   United Reformed Church
WCC   World Council of Churches

I

Why Does Division Matter?

WHAT IS ECUMENISM?

AN ECUMENICAL IMAGE PROBLEM

Ecumenism. It's not what those in advertising call 'a yes word', in fact you could say that it has an image problem, because for many people it suggests a kind of dreadful grey sameness, obliterating all that is distinctive, interesting and beautiful about different Christian traditions. And the problem is that, as with most caricatures, there is a certain amount of truth in this description. For many people the experience of ecumenism has been clouded by long and apparently pointless meetings, the search for things that churches can do together without the fear of offending anyone and a general sense of an extra layer of 'churchy' life which everyone could well do without.

Ecumenism in England could be said to be marked by a number of characteristics:

- unevenness: patterns of ecumenical working vary tremendously from one part of the country to another;
- a fear of offending one another that keeps us from real relationships with one another; it has been said that English church life is dying of niceness;
- extra-layer disease, leading to exhausting programmes that keep us at a comfortable distance from one another;
- smaller partners' concern, that they might be swamped or taken over; fear of the loss of identity by everyone;
- display of the natural dynamic of institutions that feel themselves to be under threat or in decline;
- the enthusiasm, commitment and faithfulness of a particular group of people who have remained with the ecumenical dream through thick and, sometimes very, thin.

For some of those who are most committed to working ecumenically in England, there is a bit of a sense of being 'stuck' at the moment. Many of the Churches Together groups which grew out of the former Councils of

Churches inherited from their predecessors a kind of programmatic approach to ecumenism that can feel like a relentless treadmill for those who make the running. This kind of ecumenism brings churches together for a series of activities that are almost all additional to the lives that the individual congregations pursue apart from one another. In fact the lives of those congregations are often barely touched by the ecumenical enterprise, which may be seen as a harmless enthusiasm for those who like that kind of thing. The programme in question may include some or all of the following elements:

- the Week of Prayer for Christian Unity
- Lent groups, sometimes with hunger lunches
- a walk of witness in the shopping precinct/main square on Good Friday
- Easter Praise somewhere out of doors
- Christian Aid week
- Pentecost praise, also out of doors
- One World Week
- perhaps a series of autumn talks, by invited speakers
- carol-singing in the precinct; and
- the Week of Prayer for Christian Unity again . . .

Of course, I am offering a bit of a parody and would not wish in any way to discount the excellent and very fruitful ecumenical witness of many local groups over the last thirty years, but you will know if you are involved in an ecumenical group that is stuck on this treadmill. It is an exhausting and energy-consuming exercise, and the problem with it is that we did need activities that were safely beyond the ordinary lives of our churches in order to get to know one another on neutral territory. But now many people feel frustrated with maintaining this kind of programme, and want to move on to know one another better, and most of all to serve the needs of their community more effectively together. We need a new way of relating to one another that is less safe, which moves our relationships on and which releases the churches from this programme together in their day-to-day lives and ministry.

PERHAPS WE'VE GOT IT ALL WRONG?

There is a school of thought that argues that the description given above perfectly exemplifies why the whole ecumenical enterprise is a churchy waste of time and a serious distraction from the missionary vocation of the Church. From this perspective, the churches are seen as being like a chain of retailers selling their wares on the high street; it is more likely that the Church will reach a greater number of potential consumers by being accessible through a variety of outlets, with differing styles and types of Christianity on offer. In this view, potential Christians will want to choose the brand that best suits their temperament, age and needs, and a variety of outlets is most likely to meet this varied demand. It must be taken seriously, but I find this view profoundly worrying for three reasons:

1 It seems attractive. The experience of post-modernism has encouraged people to feel that no belief system should be discounted, but that everything can be held together as being of equal virtue, offering everyone the chance to choose a religious style that is appropriate for them. We can only be grateful if this encourages people to be more tolerant, but it does present considerable problems in the search for unity, since in this view it is rather unimportant that the churches are structurally divided from one another. Their diversity is a virtue in itself, and their division only really an administrative inconvenience, if that. In this view, the brokenness of the Church is not seen as sinful, impeding or contrary to the will of God, because the Church already lives, in the power of the Spirit, in a true but invisible unity and because the Church, in its institutional form, is not seen as having a particularly important place in the economy of salvation.

2 It is based on an idea of working for unity that is distorted, but which was formed partly as a result of encounters with programmatic ecumenism (see above) and with the myth of a search for uniformity (the kind of ecumenical working that is about trying to make everyone the same, preferably just like me, whoever I am). I continue to hope that no one thinks that working for unity is working for uniformity, but I continue to encounter people outside the ecumenical conversation who do, and who are often very angry with ecumenists as a result of this misconception.

3 It threatens to undermine the Church of England's ecumenical commitment. A few years ago, there was a kind of consensus that working together in co-operation was generally a good thing and that if that developed into commitment to one another then that was an even better thing. Although the great ecumenical vision of full, visible unity is still on the horizon, and is carefully set out every time we list our priorities, there is

some reluctance to spend time on the undoubtedly tedious practicalities of travelling towards it together. Few people can find the energy to face the hard issues of Christian disunity unless they find our divisions offensive, and unless they also hold on to a vision of our unity where the Holy Spirit is at work.

SO WHY DOES DIVISION MATTER?

In *Growing Together* I want to look at the important questions around the dividedness of the Church that link our brokenness, as God's instrument of healing, with that of the human communities that we are called to serve, and at the imperatives that draw us on in the journey towards that unity in Christ which is both God's gift and the Church's calling. And I want to offer some practical suggestions for working together, based on the experience of groups of Christians engaging with their local communities who have asked, together, the question: 'What does it mean to be the people of God in this place?'

PUTTING WORKING FOR UNITY IN CONTEXT

THE LAMBEG DRUM

Recently, I was sitting in a Bible study and prayer group in the tiny hut that is the church where my husband, Jonathan, was then the minister. We read a passage from Galatians together, and then discussed it, sharing insights from our work and lives and seeking illumination from the text. Afterwards we prayed, silently at first, and then with petitions for one another, for others we knew, for the town and its churches and for peace. Rebecca, a medic, prayed,

> Lord, please help us not to rise to the taunts from the children, please help them to find a better way, and better things to do than throwing stones and petrol bombs at us. Let them not grow up learning hate and fear of those who are different, but who are their neighbours.

And John, a soldier who comes from the local area, said, 'I've been reading in Ephesians that in Christ there is neither man nor woman, Jew nor Greek, slave nor free. Lord, teach us that in you there is neither Orange nor Green.'

Jonathan has been working as an army chaplain stationed in Northern Ireland, and in that context it is not hard to locate the ways in which the churches have been identified with particular political, cultural and social divisions in society. As I write this, I can hear someone practising the Lambeg drum, on the Loyalist housing estate behind our house. For some people here, its beat speaks of bands and processions, of colour and music and a good day out with like-minded friends from the Unionist community, in the parades which take place all over the province during the summer. For others, the beat of the Lambeg drum sounds like a warning to Nationalists: Go inside and close the door. It sounds intimidatory, deep and menacing. And in this context, these two distinctive political, cultural and social identities are also inextricably linked with religious identity so that, whether the churches like it or not, they are caught up in the dividedness of the human community in a very obvious way.

In Northern Ireland, ecumenism has an even more unsteady reputation than in England, because for many people it represents the sell-out, the surrender of identity or aspiration, the willingness to compromise on ideals that others have thought worth dying for. Those called to work ecumenically in Northern Ireland have, of course, another perspective: if the primary divisions between the churches are doctrinal and theoretical – questions of the theology of the Church, Scripture, salvation, sacraments and ministry – their expression is painfully human and practical. And many of the churches have taken up the challenge of working seriously with one another and with their communities, for reconciliation.

A part of the problem lies in the ways in which it is those things that most symbolize our sense of identity, of being ourselves that also mark our differences from one another. In this context, it might be the Lambeg drum, which represents such different things to different communities, or it might be the banners of an Orange Lodge or playing Gaelic football or supporting Celtic or speaking Irish. All these are non-religious symbols, which nevertheless speak powerfully different messages to members of different communities. In the same way, it is sometimes the very things that make us feel most at home in our tradition that also make others feel most alienated when they encounter them; it might be the scent of incense as you enter the church, the presence of statues of beloved saints, or a particular tradition of preaching, or style of extemporary prayer, or singing certain hymns or songs or using the Book of Common Prayer. All these things represent the riches and treasures of a diversity of ways of responding to the same Christian faith, different ways of expressing participation in the work of the gospel. Each of them seems profoundly familiar to some of us, and profoundly strange to others.

Working for unity in Northern Ireland is extraordinarily difficult;

indeed the challenges faced by the churches there make any difficulties in the English context fade into insignificance. But it is just that profound difficulty which points to the profound importance of this work. Whenever we struggle with our dividedness as churches, we also struggle with divisions in the human community that are older and wider and deeper than the divisions of the Church, and in many cases these are divisions with which the churches are implicated. In the English context, these are less sharply defined than in Northern Ireland, but not less real.

WHAT DIVIDES US?

The churches in England are divided by many things that have little to do with theology, although our divisions are generally described along theological lines and there are important theological differences between us. However, the existence of these theological differences can also mask other divisions, which are often more ancient than even the divisions between the churches. And however diligently we search for resolutions for these theological differences, if we fail to address our other kinds of dividedness, then all our work will be in vain; and more, we will have failed to be God's instrument of healing and reconciliation in a divided world. Naming and addressing these other divisions is difficult, as they have to do with things like social class, race, geography and history, recent and ancient, which we may find hard to discuss. They are also sometimes connected with particular personalities in local churches, or with political loyalties or culture. These kinds of divisions are harder to pin down than differences over, say, infant baptism, but they can be just as important in impeding the mission of the Church and its response to God's call to become a sign and instrument of unity. Of course, in recent years increased geographical and social mobility have broken down some of these barriers, as people now move so much more easily between different Christian traditions, as they move house and job. But these divisions in the human community continue to mark and divide our lives as churches, and in some cases we have little to be proud of or complacent about, as we have mirrored and perhaps exacerbated the divisions of the human community.

Here are five examples:

In a rural–industrial market town, the railway provides a dividing line within the community: to the north are large and prosperous houses, built by those who owned or managed the mines that were once the main employer in the town. Most of these people were Church of England. To the south of the railway are smaller streets, built for those who worked in the mines. Most of these people were Methodist. Although the mines are long gone, and relationships between the churches are cordial, there is still a division along lines of class in this community, and between its churches.

In a south London suburb, a Church of England building is shared by two other congregations, who rent the building for their worship on Sunday afternoon and Sunday evening, respectively. One is an independent, black majority church, which worships in a Pentecostal tradition; the other is an African church, based in the Nigerian community. All three congregations are polite but suspicious towards one another. In the 1950s, black families from the Caribbean first began to move into the area, and they sought out those churches in which they had been brought up and worshipped at home – mostly Anglican, Methodist and Roman Catholic. They were not welcomed by the existing congregations, and felt hurt and betrayed. They met together for worship and formed a small church, which has grown into a thriving congregation. Later, during the 1970s, Nigerian families began to move into the area, bringing different traditions of worship and ethnicity. They had little in common with either of the existing congregations, both of whom were, in turn, rather suspicious of them. Now all three groups share the building that they all need, but their contacts with one another are limited to conversations about light bulbs and cleaning. Race and ethnicity continue to divide these churches from one another.

In a Midlands county, the legacy of the Commonwealth period in the seventeenth century is marked by a number of fine Congregationalist chapels with the date 1662 over the door. The congregations who built these chapels were prosperous merchants and mill owners, who also built woollen mills down the valleys, taking advantage of the plentiful supply of water and of the local sheep farms. Most of the workers at the mills worshipped in the chapels. The mills are all long gone, but the chapels remain, and few chose to join the URC when it was formed in 1972. In the surrounding agricultural area, from the seventeenth and eighteenth century onward, some of the largest farms were owned by Baptist farmers who built chapels in their villages, which most of their workers attended. The Church of England churches in these villages are rather small and unadorned, and in one village the parish church fell down during the eighteenth century, and was not rebuilt for 140 years! A few miles to the east is the estate of a great Anglican landowner. All the parish churches in these villages are large and beautifully kept, and were attended by the estate tenants and workers. These three situations all lie within a fifteen-mile radius, and the patterns of denominational allegiance are still marked by history.

In the south-west of England, two market towns within a few miles of one another remain suspicious of each other, as a result of the long-remembered hatreds and divisions of the English Civil War. Recently the relationship between the two communities has warmed, and they held some joint celebrations for the millennium; the churches have played a leading role in this growing reconciliation.

In the north-west of England, the memories of persecution and martyrdom remain for many in the Roman Catholic community, with its long history of recusancy. In a seaside town, two parishes – Church of England and Roman Catholic – are working towards building a new church, which will provide them with a common home. Both congregations are large and flourishing, with a shared focus on mission and service. They have worked together through some of the bitter feelings about their histories, and in naming those things have been able to express their repentance and move on in their relationship. We are all products of our history, but we are not obliged to be its victims.

Exercise 1.1: In Your Own Community

Take a few minutes to note your responses to the following questions:

• In your local area, what other factors, apart from doctrinal questions, can you identify as dividing the churches?
• What kinds of things divide your community?
• Which aspects of your tradition are most important to you?
• Are there things which you find strange or difficult in other traditions?

IDENTITY AND BELONGING

There are few emotions in human experience as powerful as the sense of feeling at home, of knowing yourself to be among your own people, among familiar surroundings and with people who share a common language and history, whose attitudes and beliefs have been shaped by similar experience. To be at home is to be comfortable and safe, known and understood. When you are far from home the longing to be there can be almost overwhelming. When you enter your home, there are certain things, many of them subconscious, which make you feel at home – familiar objects and scents, things that you have chosen or have had for a long time, perhaps things that you have inherited from a previous generation. For many people, the experience of entering their church has many of the same characteristics – it reinforces their sense of being on home territory, in the company of those who are like them; it has familiar objects and scents, and things that mark the passage of time from one generation to another. These familiar things – the kind of furniture and the way in which it is arranged, the particular translation of Scripture, the presence of statues, an organ, familiar hymns, patterns of church life, worship and liturgy – are often the same in churches of a particular tradition across the country, even across the world. So when we are away from our geographical home, the home of our tradition is still available to us, reassuring and comforting, telling us that here we will find people who are like ourselves.

In a way there is nothing wrong with this comforting reinforcement of our sense of identity and belonging, but it does have an accompanying danger. During the twentieth century, there were many examples of the peril of carrying this longing to be with and governed by those who are like you into the fear and hatred of those who are different. Whenever we define ourselves by what makes us different from others, we are in danger of travelling a road that leads to some terrible places; even to the exclusion and persecution of those who are different from us.

ALPHABETS IN FORMER YUGOSLAVIA

One of the more obvious distinctions between nationalities in Europe is shown in the use of alphabets. When Jonathan was serving as a chaplain to the British Army in Bosnia, he travelled through many places where the Serb, Croat and Muslim communities had formerly lived peacefully together, but one or other had been driven out by warfare or 'ethnic cleansing'. Signposts in mixed areas of former Yugoslavia used to bear names in both the Cyrillic alphabet used by Serbs, and the Roman alphabet used by others, but one of the marks of ethnic imperialism was the obliteration of one form or its overlaying by another. Sometimes this involved the restitution of an older name; the town that had been called Duvno (Wind) under Tito reverted to being called Tomislavgrad, in honour of the medieval Croatian king, which was a source of rejoicing to the majority population but of intimidation to the Muslim minority. Similarly, as soon as the Serbian forces had left Kosovo a number of signs had their Cyrillic names defaced and overlaid with Albanian forms as an overt act of triumphalism.

In the relative peace and comfort of England, it can be easy to dismiss this kind of experience as being very distant from our own – to tell ourselves that this could never happen here. But it did happen recently, in our own continent and time, and to people who only a few years before had been living together peacefully, if not in harmony.

We are all part of a complex, rich, multicultural context in Britain; we should not be blind to our own prejudices and subconscious feelings towards those whom we see as 'different', whether racially, culturally or in terms of physical or mental health.

There is a paradox in that the proper and reasonable longing for a sense of identity and belonging, which is made even more alluring by our divided and fragmented society, and the things that offer us a sense of being at home, which speak to us of community and coherence, are also the things which can lead us to reject those who are different, and with them real community, and all the gifts which God has for his Church and for a divided world, where we are called together to be agents of healing and liberation.

Exercise 1.2: Sharing Spiritual Treasures

Often we may assume that our ecumenical partners know and understand us and our traditions, so that we do not need to explain ourselves. Or we may assume that we know and understand them, but are actually referring to stereotypes, or to a way of being that belongs to another age. Or we may use the same language to describe different ideas and experiences, or different language to describe ideas and experiences that are very similar. People often find it hardest to talk about those things that are really important to them (which is perhaps why British people all spend so much time talking about the weather) and this may especially be the case around questions of faith or Christian tradition. Sometimes we hesitate to speak for fear of offending those from other traditions, when actually what is lost is the opportunity for all to be enriched and perhaps challenged by our diversity. This kind of sharing is just as important a part of growing into friendship as washing up in other people's church kitchens, and often grows out of the experience of working together in practical things, and so coming to want to get to know one another on a deeper level.

Plan a session lasting one to two hours, for a house group or evening meeting, in which you and others from your church could share some of the aspects of your tradition that are important to you. What are the treasures of your tradition, in worship, spirituality, church life? How could you enable others to discover them?

The Churches Together in England Spirituality Co-ordinating Group have produced an excellent resource leaflet called *Sharing Spiritual Treasures*, which makes some suggestions for creating an atmosphere in which people feel free to share what really matters to them about their faith, and are also free to receive the gifts brought by those from other traditions.

Sharing Spiritual Treasures is about:

- sharing stories and experience;
- appreciating our different traditions; and
- finding nourishment for our faith.

This is a resource best used in groups of six to eight people, so that everyone has the opportunity to contribute. It might be helpful in enabling members of an existing ecumenical group to share with one another on a deeper level, or as a first step for people who are used to working together in practical things but not to talking about their faith together. The Spirituality Co-ordinating Group offers the following guidelines for the group.

- Create a warm, friendly, expectant atmosphere. A focal point may be helpful, perhaps the objects brought by the group.
- Agree the time and length of the meeting. Ensure each person has time to speak.
- Encourage people to contribute as and when they feel appropriate and agree to keep confidentiality.
- Let the group listen and receive what is said in silence: remind people that this is not a discussion.

- After everyone has spoken, there may be silent or shared reflection.
- Allow time for the group to consider whether it would like to meet again.

Bring to the meeting something which is significant for you, and which you want to share. It might be:

- an object, important for itself or for the memories it evokes;
- a verse or two from the Bible;
- a hymn, poem or piece of music;
- a photograph, picture or icon; or
- a memory of a person or event.

Say why the contribution you have brought is important to you (share only what you want to). Then:

- Listen to other people without comment.
- Reflect on the spiritual treasures that people have shared. How do they relate to your own experiences?
- Consider, as a group, whether you would like to meet again for other opportunities to share your faith journeys.

Copies of the leaflet *Sharing Spiritual Treasures* are available from Churches Together in England.

DIVERSITY AND DIVISION

Discovering and enjoying one another's spiritual traditions in their diversity does not, however, mean ignoring or minimizing our differences or making light of the divisions between us. The diversity of the churches is a delightful thing, reflecting the transmission of the gospel through a variety of contexts, histories, geographies, reforms and cultures. The dividedness of the churches is another matter altogether; this dividedness is a state of sin, a state of being less than the Church in our separation. In our divisions we sometimes reject one another as being expressions of the life of the Church and seek, when we do relate to one another, to remake one another in our own image.

For many years working for unity has been caricatured as working for uniformity, as if the longing for visible unity meant the reduction of all our traditions into a bland muddle of those aspects of each least likely to offend others. This sort of 'ecumenism' is rather like eating overcooked porridge: tasty and delicious ingredients have been poured into the pot and boiled together for many hours until all that made them delicious is reduced to an inoffensive beige mess. This kind of approach to working together, which is occasionally encountered in the saddest kind of ecumenical worship, is best consigned to the bin as being dull, unappetizing, lacking in nourishment and unlikely to appeal to anyone, however hungry. This is not really what ecumenism is about. Ecumenism is about encountering difference and embracing the other, about seeking that which we hold in common and enjoying the different ways in which God has mediated his gospel through the experience of the Church down the ages. This kind of unity is rather about setting on the table a wonderfully varied and delicious feast – the feast of all the flavours and scents, tastes and textures of our different traditions. The feast is set on the table of God's generosity, and in his household, which is that temple to which Paul refers in the Letter to the Ephesians:

> So he came and proclaimed peace to you who were far off and peace to those who were near; for through him both of us have access in one Spirit to the Father. So then you are no longer strangers and aliens, but you are citizens with the saints and also members of the household of God, built upon the foundation of the apostles and prophets, with Christ Jesus himself as the cornerstone. In Him the whole structure is joined together and grows into a holy temple in the Lord; in whom you also are built together spiritually into a dwelling-place for God.
>
> (Ephesians 2.17–22, NRSV)

One of the ways of translating the word *oikumene* from the Greek is as God's 'householding' of the whole creation, so that the links between the table that the Church sets and the house where it stands are particularly strong. At this table there is a place for everyone and enough for all to eat and be satisfied. This is the table to which we invite the hungry and the excluded, and where we ourselves find nourishment for the work, as we are built up into a dwelling place for God.

So working for unity is far from working for uniformity, but it is about taking division seriously, as the tables on which we serve this feast are broken tables. As all creation reflects the delight of the Creator in diversity and variety, so our traditions reflect a thousand ways of responding to and passing on the gospel. Living in unity does not mean all being the same or all becoming the same, but it does mean our coming to recognize our need of one another. As God is at work in the history of the Church and of humankind, so

through the years of our division the different traditions have
guarded different ways of telling and living the gospel, different
kinds of liturgical tradition, spirituality, patterns of church life and
approaches to pastoral care. To become the Church together we need
each other, as each of us has what the other lacks.

Exercise 1.3

Here is a quotation from the theologian Rowan Williams, who is
Archbishop of Wales.

> We have to learn to live as if we could not move towards God
> without the gift of one another, in the recognition that my healing
> and my freedom are only thinkable in union with the healing and
> freedom of all, and that my liberation commits me to the creation
> of the kind of community in which all can be involved in nurtur-
> ing and re-creating one another, in the power of God's Spirit.
>
> (Williams, 1990)

Use it for some quiet reflection on the questions:

- What have I learnt from those of other traditions which has
  inspired and encouraged me on my journey?
- How is God challenging me to receive other Christians as gifts?

It is a particular feature of the life of the Church in this country that
we have a tremendous variety of ecumenical partners, and also a
reasonable balance of numbers, so that there are few places where we
do not have the opportunity to work with Christians of other traditions. While not every settlement in England has a selection of places
of worship of various kinds, most of us find ourselves working with
or living alongside Christians from different traditions and discovering more about different ways of being the Church and of being a
Christian from our relationships with them. This is sometimes
referred to as the different traditions in Christianity being gifts,
from God, to one another. I always find the idea of those who are
different as gifts to one another quite a challenging one; sometimes
when you open a gift you find that what is inside is not what you had
expected, and others may see as gifts in our tradition things that we
ourselves find difficult and unappealing.

Although there are places in England where the memory of persecution and religious intolerance is still strong, in most places we

have had an opportunity that has been denied to many of our partners in other European contexts; that of developing our relationship with one another in an atmosphere of comparative peace, tolerance and religious freedom for at least the past century. This maturity of relationship across a variety of traditions gives us a particular opportunity but also a particular responsibility – to make the most of our context and to grow in our relationships with one another beyond painting the fences between us and being polite to one another across them.

UNITY AND TELLING THE TRUTH

One of the most encouraging features of ecumenical life in England is the maturity of the relationships between the churches: recent years have brought a number of issues and situations that have challenged the churches and stretched our relationships with one another, but the bonds between us have proved to be stronger than these difficulties. For example, churches that have ordained women to the ministry of word and sacrament continue in close relationship with those that have not, and we have been able to talk about this issue with one another, and to share our pains and our experience, even work together to help those who have left one church and joined another in response to this development. This does not mean that the ordination of women is irrelevant to ecumenical dialogue, but that the relationships between the churches have been tested and have withstood the developments in one another's lives, and in areas where developments could have presented further reasons for division. However, for the churches to gain the benefits of this mature relationship it is essential that our ecumenical relationships are based in the truth about ourselves; as in all areas of human relating, relationships based on illusion and pretence are not really relationships, as within them we are not truly ourselves. But with those with whom our friendship is mature and of long standing, we can reveal something of our vulnerability without fear of rejection or betrayal.

Telling the truth about ourselves and our traditions has a number of important implications for the ways in which we relate to one another. Often when we first meet those from other churches, we are anxious to show our own in the best possible light – thriving, full of young people, rich in spirituality and financially secure. Just as in our personal relationships, it is usually only with those whom we know well that we admit our fears about the future, our decline in numbers or other difficulties. I have spoken elsewhere in this book about the ecumenical pain barrier, and one of the ways in which we know that we have passed through it and discovered a new quality of relationship is when we are able to share with partner churches the difficult truths about the life of our own.

Another aspect of this ecumenical truthfulness is revealed in the ways in which we present our churches to one another. It is exceedingly tempting, when forming a relationship with another church, to show the side of your tradition that is most like theirs. This might seem a good way to begin the relationship, but unless we can share the truth about our traditions, in all their multicoloured glory, then the relationship is not really based in our tradition as we have received it, and as it perhaps has that which our partner lacks. This kind of approach requires us to work at our relationships with one another – it takes us beyond a superficial acquaintance and the stereotyped views that we tend to begin with and into a quite different kind of relationship, where we truly listen to one another as we truly speak about ourselves. Courtesy is an indispensable value in ecumenical relationships, but there is also a dreadful kind of politeness that prevents us from being real with one another. Where relationships between the churches flourish, they are truthful relationships, in which people are able to be themselves, and to express fully their own traditions, and not a watered-down version.

This truthfulness in our ecumenical relationships also requires a large measure of charity towards one another and a quality of listening to one another as we share our traditions, confident that God has been at work in the experience of other churches and is at work in our developing relationship. Being open with one another about things that are profoundly important to us can be rather difficult in British culture, where it may be a mark of something being profoundly important that it is never mentioned. As our relationships with one another mature, they may be characterized by:

- a growing expectation that the partnership is a place where the Holy Spirit is at work;
- being open with one another and therefore vulnerable to one another and to God and to renewal together;
- a willingness to be changed in our experience of working for unity, just as we are changed by all the relationships of our lives;
- a creativity in response to our shared context for mission;

- a focusing on the needs of the place which we are called to serve;
- an outward-looking relationship that responds to the priority kingdom – world – church;
- a lively vision that we are more than the sum of our parts, and that in growing together we are not watering down our traditions, but rather enriching them.

This kind of mature, truthful relationship is developed over years and requires truthful listening as well as truthful speaking. Some of the things which our partners need to say to us will be hard to hear, and may concern the wrongs that we have done them in the past and may be doing them in the present. But as churches learn to speak the truth about themselves and to one another, they grow together into a new quality of relationship and in a new quality of witness and service to the place they are called to serve.

THE ECOLOGY OF UNITY

When thinking about different ways of working for unity and different understandings of the aim of that work, various different models of the unity of the Church are sometimes used, for example:

- *unity in reconciled diversity*: the preservation of distinctive gifts within continuing denominations, reconciled with one another and taking counsel together;
- *unity in solidarity*: unity that is sought not only in doctrine but in the struggle against evil and injustice;
- *a communion of communions*: united but not absorbed, communions would retain many distinctive features but live in communion with a universal primate;
- *federal unity*: traditions continue with full autonomy, but covenant to co-operate together;
- *conciliar fellowship*: churches, local in place and time, hold in fellowship together in councils and counsel;
- *organic unity*: separate denominations dissolve into a unity with one another that has a common structure and that reflects the gifts and traditions which are the inheritance of each of those denominations.

You may recognize one or more of these models of unity from the ecumenical activity in your own local area or church community.

I don't really find the use of such models very helpful, although it is quite useful to have a common language of ideas for describing different approaches to unity. However, language changes and develops with time, and in the years since the expression 'organic unity' was coined, our understanding of the concept of 'organic' has developed tremendously. Where once it may have had rather organizational connotations, in the popular sense 'organic' now refers to something natural or green, something rather wholesome but also dynamic, connected with growth and green shoots. I find it helpful to think in terms of a kind of ecology of unity, where unity is the natural state of the Church, and is something into which we grow together, as we grow towards God. This growth, however, is not a painless process, as the Vinedresser will prune this vine to encourage stronger growth and greater fruitfulness. And the test of our unity is always our fruitfulness: Is the gospel proclaimed in the way in which we are the Church, together? Not in what we say or even do, but in how we are? Are we communities of healing and liberation, bearing the fruits of the Spirit and renewed as we grow together?

Often in the history of the churches, breaking into disunity has been consequent on the rejection of renewal, as the Church has been unable to contain new insights and challenges within the body. The history of the development of Methodism within the Church of England is one such example. If unity is the fruit of the Spirit at work in the Church, how might we be renewed together, for mission, in ways in which we might not be renewed in our separation from one another and from God? This unity is the gift of God to the Church, but it is also the calling of the Church to discover unity, to receive it and to search for it by living and working together in witness and service and in the faith which we already share. In Chapters 3 and 4, we will go on to look at some examples of churches living together in these ways.

HORIZONTAL AND VERTICAL ECUMENISM

One important question remains, before we close this chapter. Are the significant divisions between the churches or within them? In talking about ecumenical relationships, we are used to thinking about the divisions between different Christian traditions, but most of us have had the experience of relating to those from different traditions who seem closer to us than others from our own church. These different kinds of division are sometimes described as horizontal and vertical differences. The divisions between the churches, which we are accustomed to think of as the business of the ecumenical movement, can be understood as vertical, while other strands, which cross different Christian traditions, can be seen as horizontal:

Congregationalist   Lutheran   Methodist   URC   Anglican   Baptist   RC

Sacramentalist
Charismatic renewal
Liberalism
Social gospel
Julian spirituality
Liberation theologies
Radical Christianity
Shared locality
Pacifism
Evangelicalism
Approaches to Scripture
Conservatism

The list is almost endless . . .

This understanding of the churches challenges us to admit both the ways in which we are divided from those in our own tradition and the ways in which we are sometimes closer to those from other traditions, with whom we share common insights and experiences. These divisions often also need healing, as the limits of diversity are stretched within our own church. So that, for example, a Roman Catholic and a Baptist who have both been influenced by the charismatic movement, or an Anglican and a Methodist with a strong sacramental devotion, or people from any number of traditions who live or work in the same place, might have a closer experience of fellowship with one another than with others from their own tradition. This makes conventional ecumenical relationships both easier and much more complicated; it certainly adds to the complex and variegated picture that is ecumenical life in England, and these complexities cannot be ignored if we are to make progress in growing together both within our traditions and across them.

2

Who Are Your Partner Churches?

DEVELOPING RELATIONSHIPS

Over the last twenty years, the ecumenical structures in Britain and Ireland have undergone a transformation, as a result of a vision of ecumenism, which is not an extra, but a dimension of all that we do. This vision was born of a number of factors and circumstances:

- a growing recognition that the British Council of Churches (BCC), founded in 1942, was no longer as effective an instrument as it could be, partly because it was insufficiently tied into the lives and cultures of the churches, so that the good work done by BCC staff sometimes had little impact on the churches as institutions;
- the visit of the Pope, in 1982, which proved a catalyst for an intensification of ecumenical relations, especially with the Roman Catholic Church, which was at that time an observer rather than a full member of the BCC;
- the failure of the Covenant for Unity, also in 1982, which provided an impetus for development on a broader front.

These factors, together with the growth in working for unity in local communities, provided the opportunity for a fresh approach at all levels, and the churches worked together, through the Inter-Church Process, *Not Strangers but Pilgrims* in 1985, and the Lent course, *What on Earth is the Church for?* in 1986, to discover what kind of structures were now appropriate to support working for unity, and what kind of vision of unity the churches now shared. This wide-ranging consultative process was a brave step for the churches, as those working for unity at every level were included, and over one million people took part. It turned out to be a revelatory experience, as the depth and intensity of ecumenical working was revealed, along with a frustration with both the partner churches and the ecumenical structures on the part of those working locally.

In 1987, the representatives from churches in Britain and Ireland met at Swanwick and, bringing together the results of the Inter-Church Process and reflecting on them, agreed that the way forward was a new way of working that called the churches to:

> declare together our readiness to commit ourselves to each other under God . . . It is our conviction that, as a matter of policy at all levels and in all places, our churches must now move from co-operation to clear commitment to one another, in search for the unity for which Christ prayed and in common evangelism and service of the world.
>
> (Swanwick Declaration, 1987)

In this shift of thinking, the churches accepted that they would be challenged to participate more intensively in working for unity; the BCC agreed to make way for new structures that would better facilitate this new way of working, and these new ecumenical instruments were inaugurated in 1990:

- the Council of Churches for Britain and Ireland (CCBI), now Churches Together in Britain and Ireland (CTBI);
- Action of Churches Together in Scotland (ACTS);
- Churches Together in Wales (Cytun);
- in Ireland, the Irish Council of Churches continued, along with the Ballymascanlon process, which enabled contact with the Roman Catholic Bishops' Conference;
- Churches Together in England (CTE).

CHURCHES TOGETHER IN BRITAIN AND IRELAND

At CTBI, work on agenda areas is undertaken through commissions, networks and agencies. All this work is all focused on co-ordinating and bringing together the priorities and work of the partner churches, in areas such as public affairs, international relations and church life. The constituent parts of CTBI meet every two years for an assembly, and between assemblies the work is sustained through the Church Representatives' Meeting.

CHURCHES TOGETHER IN ENGLAND

The Churches Together in England meet every two years for a forum, which includes representatives from groupings between the national and local levels – the Intermediate level.

The CTE Enabling Group brings together those who are appointed to represent their churches, to take counsel together with:

- those who represent bodies in association with the instrument, such as the Association of Inter-Church Families;
- co-ordinating groups, such as the Group for Local Unity, and the Theology and Unity Group;
- agencies, such as Christian Aid or the Christian Enquiry Agency; and
- representatives from the regions of England and from the CTE Forum.

ACTION OF CHURCHES TOGETHER IN SCOTLAND

ACTS is based at Scottish Churches House, Dunblane, and meets every few years in a very large Scottish Christian gathering. The member churches are brought together through a central council and their work together is served by commissions, committees, networks and agencies. ACTS also encourages local ecumenical working through Local Ecumenical Partnerships and Churches Together groups. Some of the member churches are also engaged in the Scottish Churches Initiative for Union (SCIFU).

CYTUN ('Together')

In Wales Cytun succeeded the Council of Churches for Wales and brings together the churches for *Y Gymanfa* ('a gathering') once every two years. In between these assemblies the relationship between the churches is co-ordinated by a steering committee and council, and their work is enabled through commissions and networks. In Wales there is also a Covenant for Union (Enfys – 'rainbow') which was established in 1975 between the Church in Wales, the Presbyterian Church of Wales, the Methodist Church, the United Reformed Church and the Covenanted Baptist Churches. Both Cytun and Enfys promote local initiatives for unity, through Churches Together groups and Local Ecumenical Partnerships.

The most important characteristic of the post-1990 ecumenical structures in Britain and Ireland remains that they exist to enable effective working for unity in mission and service by the churches together, and not as an end in themselves.

In 2001, the life of CTE developed yet again, as the Free Churches Council (FCC) became a part of the national instrument, and CTE took on a wider agenda, which includes some of the former FCC work.

COUNTY AND METROPOLITAN AREA CHURCHES TOGETHER

Almost every county and every metropolitan area now has a Churches Together grouping, to enable co-operation between the churches at that level of their lives – between the very local and the national – which is known as the 'Intermediate level'. Just as work at the very local level is immensely varied, so these Intermediate bodies are also varied in their level of resources and staffing and in their effectiveness. Most are served by a county ecumenical officer (CEO) or secretary, but these posts may be full time, part time or spare time, and are sometimes combined with the responsibilities of a denominational ecumenical officer and perhaps also with pastoral ministry. At the Intermediate level, the churches share a complex common agenda that encompasses the oversight, review and development of Local Ecumenical Partnerships (LEPs) and local Churches Together groups; planning together; sponsoring joint work in social responsibility, further education chaplaincy or local broadcasting; sharing ideas and developments from each church and looking at questions of deployment and resources. Where Intermediate bodies work well, the agenda which they share is the churches' agenda, and the churches bring to the table matters of importance to them in their own lives.

For those working for unity in local communities, the Intermediate level is an important source of information and encouragement, and CEOs, who often work in a team with the denominational ecumenical officers (DEOs), are the first place to look for support and ideas.

The Intermediate level is still a relatively new level for working together. Until the late 1970s there were just a few places, mostly large cities, where the local Council of Churches had employed an officer to enable their working for unity. As the numbers of LEPs grew, so sponsoring bodies were developed to provide a suitable structure to enable the parent churches to share in oversight. These two kinds of bodies gradually developed into the pattern of county Churches Together.

CHURCH LEADERS' MEETINGS AND CHURCH LEADERS' COVENANTS

An important aspect of working together at the Intermediate level in many areas is a church leaders' meeting, which usually brings together the Church of England and Roman Catholic bishops (or an archdeacon or vicar general representing them), the Methodist

District chairman, the United Reformed Church provincial synod moderator and a member of the Baptist leadership team. These people, sometimes together with a regional Salvation Army commander, clearly represent the very different understandings of the ministry of oversight of the partner churches, and this highlights a continuing difficulty in representing churches to one another. However, many church leaders' meetings provide a helpful opportunity to share with colleagues and friends who also carry the burden of oversight, and the church leaders' meeting is also an expression of ecumenical collegiality.

In some areas there are also regional meetings of church leaders, either across the range of partner churches or bilaterally; for example, Anglican and Roman Catholic bishops meet in the West Midlands region.

In many places there is also a church leaders' covenant, which is a personal expression of commitment to working for unity by the group of church leaders, sometimes also ratified by the synodical structures of their churches. In such covenants, the church leaders commit themselves to work for unity through meeting, praying and taking counsel together, in their ministries of oversight. Because of their personal nature, covenants are often renewed when new church leaders are appointed, and they usually cover the area of an Intermediate body, so one church leader might be signatory to several covenants. There is also one regional Church Leaders' Covenant, in the north-east of England.

A useful book on the Intermediate level is *This Growing Unity: A Handbook on Ecumenical Development in the Counties, Large Cities and New Towns of England* by Roger Nunn (CTE Publications, 1995).

WORKING TOGETHER IN THE ENGLISH REGIONS

Since 1997, the English regions have become an increasingly important unit for government, and the churches have developed regional structures, where they were not already present, in order to participate appropriately at this level. In some regions, the churches also work with other faith communities, as the regional structures provide for one representative for them all. In some regions – for example, the North-West and the North-East – the churches have appointed a regional officer, to enable and co-ordinate their participation in regional government. The agenda at regional level is principally focused on economic and social regeneration, and the churches' participation is usually as one of a number of voluntary organizations or interest groups.

CHURCHES TOGETHER AND COUNCILS OF CHURCHES

The existence of councils of churches in local communities dates back to the end of the First World War, but most were set up in the period following the establishment of the British Council of Churches. These local groups – some established formally with constitutions and committees, some rather more informal, and varying greatly in size – are by far the greatest part of the work being undertaken for unity in England, and there are well over a thousand such groups.

In many communities they are now local Churches Together groups, some of which are called Christians Together, while others have held on to their identity as councils of churches. The principle behind the change of name here is the same as in the national instruments: to move beyond sustaining a round of ecumenical life that is apart from the lives of the churches, and instead to bring those lives together, enabling the churches to share their daily experience of faith, life and witness with one another.

For some Churches Together, the change of name has been just that, and their ecumenical programme has continued undisturbed; the sadness about some of these situations is that working for unity is unlikely, in these places, to bring the churches closer either to one another or to the communities within which they are set. This kind of ecumenical working is often perceived as the province of those who are enthusiasts, rather than the business of the whole Church, and as energy-consuming rather than energy-releasing. Most local areas, however, need to spend time in this kind of relationship, while people get to know one another on the neutral territory which an extra round of ecumenical life creates. Eventually their relationship comes to a maturity where the round of special events is no longer necessary, and where they can move into a new phase of life together. Recognizing when this stage has been reached and moving into the new phase is not easy. Letting go of a round of events can feel like the end of ecumenism, and ecumenical groups can sometimes represent an alternative power base for those who are disenfranchised in their own churches, and who may be reluctant to hand on the task of representation to those who are able to speak for their church with authority. The work of those who have maintained the relationships between the churches for many years must be acknowledged, and sometimes it is those very people who see the need to move to a different way of working.

In the heady optimism of the new beginnings for the ecumenical instruments in 1990, few people realized what a long process of change they were part of. Work for unity in Britain does proceed at very different speeds and in very different ways in different places; in some local areas the transformation of the ecumenical structures has still yet to begin, while in others those working for unity already feel that they have reached the limits of the new structures, and are hungry to move on to another stage of yet-closer unity. What the post-1990 structures do encourage is making decisions and taking steps together by consensus: under the earlier structures – where decisions were sometimes made by majority voting – the people involved may have felt that it was easier to 'get things done', but this sometimes resulted in a lack of support for ecumenical initiatives by some of the partner churches, and would not have been a pattern of life that, for example, the Roman Catholic Church would have felt able to join. Many Churches Together groups found a renewal of energy in the changes following the Inter-Church Process, as other churches became full partners in the ecumenical enterprise, and brought with them new insights and a fresh approach.

The former structures enabled us to become friends, and sometimes to act together: they maintained our relationships through some very eventful and sometimes difficult periods, especially following the failures of the Anglican–Methodist Union Scheme in 1972 and the Covenant for Unity between the Methodist Church, the Moravian Church, the United Reformed Church and the Church of England in 1982. The aim of the post-1990 structures is not only to sustain our relationships, but to make them easier to join for new partners and, ultimately, to transform the lives of the participating churches, as they grow closer to one another. In many communities, this transformation is closely tied to their engagement with the local community, so that Churches Together have asked, together: What does it mean to be the people of God in this place? And in discovering the answer together they have themselves both been transformed as a group and as churches, and have also found themselves to be agents of transformation in their communities, and discovered unity in this common task.

In talking about Churches Together groups in local communities in England, the discussion embraces an enormous variety of situations, from organizations in metropolitan boroughs that have eighty member churches and employ full-time staff, to a group of three churches in a rural area. Some of this diversity, and of the common strands of experience, is further set out in Chapter 4. An excellent resource for further reflection on this area is the book *Together Locally: A Handbook for Local Churches Seeking to Work Together* by Jenny Carpenter (CTE Publications, 1998).

MINISTERS' MEETINGS

Another ecumenical structure that has proved important in many places is the ministers' meeting or fraternal, which has often provided a place where friendship has grown, in mutual support and encouragement. In those local situations where relationships between the churches have stood the test of time, they have always extended beyond fellow feeling among the ministers to be owned by lay people, who have often proved to be the ones who have found the capacity for the lateral thinking that was necessary. Nevertheless, ministers' meetings have often proved a testing place for ecumenical working. As Churches Together groups begin to work with new partner churches that have not been part of the ecumenical structures in the past, it is important to think inclusively, so that pastors who have other employment during the day are sometimes able to attend, and so that those churches that have no identified ministers are also represented. It is also helpful to keep reminding the meeting of the importance of an appropriate relationship with the wider Churches Together structures, so that ideas and decisions are communicated between the two.

AN ECUMENICAL PAIN BARRIER?

Taken together, these structures amount to a very firm and well-constructed framework to support the churches' relationships; the way that working for unity in England is rooted in local experience is much admired by people working in other contexts. The danger of such structures is that they enable us not to be transformed together into the kind of unity to which God is calling us, but rather to live comfortably with our dividedness, which can be masked by the very structures that are supposed to promote its healing. When one of the partner churches then raises a question or asserts a point of view that others find difficult, there is often a lot of hurt and anger around.

An example of this is the Roman Catholic Bishops' Conference's document on the Eucharist, 'One Bread, One Body', published in

1999. However, what this teaching document does is remind us, rather painfully for some, of the real and continuing divisions between us – divisions that will not be healed by our hoping that they will go away. Although the document caused pain for many people – especially for those in inter-church families, ecumenical communities and partnerships – it also provided a reality check for ecumenical working. This is what the Roman Catholic Church teaches, and this is a part of the basis on which it participates in working for unity. The problem is partly that, although we know this to be the case, for many of us the ecumenical structures protect us from facing the difficult reality, and we do experience unity as a gift already received as well as a goal to be sought. But unless the whole ecumenical movement (and not only those for whom there is an obvious personal impact) manages to stay with these difficult issues, which mark our division, then we will not discover together the means for our reconciliation. The structures for our working together are there to enable us to keep talking to one another, to stay together and to work together at these difficult issues; they are also there to enable the churches to grow together in a truthful and honest relationship, and not to paint the fences which divide them, rather than dismantling those fences, piece by piece.

PARTNER CHURCHES IN ENGLAND

Because some of the patterns of working for unity are so long-established in England, it is easy to make assumptions about one another as churches, on the basis that we have known one another for a long time and therefore know one another well. However, we are often working out of stereotypes that may be based on ways of thinking and acting that belong well in the past. Below, some of the churches or groups of churches who are partners in working for unity in England set out a description of their lives as churches. This is intended to be of help to those who are working with a particular partner church for the first time, or who want to find out more about some aspect of another church. It is not intended to be a comprehensive guide to all the churches, but rather to offer a background to working for unity, and a flavour of the diversity of the churches. Included in each description is something about each of the following:

- theological basis
- ministry

- liturgy and worship
- spirituality
- church life
- structures for government, oversight and taking counsel together
- relations with world communion or family of churches
- ethos and character
- ecumenical working.

However, the material from each church is shaped by its own particular polity and priorities. See the 'Useful Sources of Information' section for further details.

THE BAPTIST UNION OF GREAT BRITAIN

THEOLOGICAL BASIS

While Baptists are best known for their particular stand on baptism and their separatist stance towards the state, it was biblical and theological refection on the nature of covenant and the new covenant community that offered the focal point for Baptist identity. Part of the impetus that moved people into a Baptist pattern of church life was the idea of the Church being a community of believers, in which matters of discipline were treated very seriously and where the community depended on the mutual commitment and submission of members one to another before God. This model of discipleship church or believers' church, into which a person entered through confession of faith and believers' baptism, was radically different from the parish system. It was not a soft option in that the covenant promise made by early Baptist communities 'to walk with each other and with God' could easily and often did culminate in a martyr's call. Still today covenant theology provides the context and logic for Baptist identity and ecclesiology, undergirding the Baptist emphasis on the priority of the local church for the mission of the gospel, and undergirding basic and deep convictions about human rights and the possibility of all to worship freely according to their conscience.

A national basis of union between Baptists was drawn up in 1813. However, by the end of the nineteenth century, when it was all too easy for different factions to go their separate ways, a much more open Declaration of Principle was adopted. The declaration was designed to hold together in covenant a wide Baptist family, rather than to create the kinds of boundaries more typically associated with a creed, which largely serve to hold people apart.

The Basis of the Union is:

1 That our Lord and Saviour Jesus Christ, God manifest in the flesh, is the sole and absolute authority in all matters relating to faith and practice, as revealed in Holy Scriptures, and that each Church has liberty under the guidance of the Holy Spirit to interpret and administer His Laws.
2 That Christian Baptism is the immersion in water into the name of the Father, Son and Holy Ghost of those who have professed repentance towards God and faith in our Lord Jesus Christ who 'died for our sins according to the scriptures: was buried and rose again the third day'.
3 That it is the duty of every disciple to bear witness to the Gospel of Jesus Christ, and to take part in the evangelisation of the world.

Theologically Baptists today would want to say that in the making of covenant be it Sinai, Calvary, or the present day, the text is always secondary to the relationship, the covenant document subordinate to the covenant promise. Our claim is that God's Covenant of grace is full of potential to enable Baptists to clarify, for themselves and others, a distinctive way of being church which is neither independent nor hierarchical. This we suggest is our proper identity within the plethora of communions in the modern world, and covenant language is a very powerful factor in its expression. We are interdependents, not independents and we locate authority in community not in hierarchy.

BAPTIST RELATIONS WITH WORLD COMMUNION OR FAMILY OF CHURCHES

The Baptist World Alliance (BWA) has a membership of some 43 million baptized believers. In numerical terms at least Baptists are a major stream within the Christian Church. Numerical strength is not equally spread geographically. The vast majority – 33 million – are in North America; 4 million in Africa and Asia; 1.5 million in Latin America; with 765,000 in Europe and the Middle East; and finally 220,000 in the Caribbean.

The BWA holds within this family a wide diversity of theological opinion. As with every world communion this diversity is a tension which at its best is a source of enrichment, but can sometimes lead to misunderstanding, division and hurt.

The Baptist Union of Great Britain (BUGB) has a long and rich history of ecumenical involvement with partner traditions in the Christian Church. Its own beginning as a union was the result of ecumenical dialogue and convergence between two strands of Baptist thinking: the General Baptists (Arminian) and the Particular Baptists (Calvinist). Within Britain the Fellowship of British Baptists brings together today into close partnership three autonomous Baptist Unions (the Baptist Union of Great Britain, the Baptist Union of Scotland and the Baptist Union of Wales). There is also a Baptist Union of Ireland which is not currently a member of this fellowship.

The Baptist Union of Great Britain has been a full member of the World Council of Churches (WCC) and Conference of European Churches (CEC) since their foundation, and Baptist leaders such as Dr Ernest Payne were among those who brought the international post-war dream of closer ecumenical co-operation into reality. Today many local Baptist churches are actively involved in local Churches Together initiatives. A significant number of these are also covenant-ed partners in Local Ecumenical Projects.

BAPTIST MINISTRY

Baptists have consistently affirmed the priesthood of all believers, which basically means every member enjoys direct access to God through prayer and service and every member is a channel or the location for God's ministry into the community.

During the 1960s, however, the notion of a set-apart ministry of word and sacrament was summed up in a document on 'the Doctrine of Ministry', which states that

> some forms of ministry are set aside by ordination usually by the laying on of hands. Ordination is the act wherein the Church under the guidance of the Holy Spirit publicly recognises and confirms that a Christian believer has been gifted, called and set apart by God for the work of the ministry and in the name of Christ commissions for this work.

While the wording of this particular document spoke of ministry in male terms, the principle of recognizing women into fully ordained ministry within the churches of the BUGB has been established for over 100 years.

During the 1990s the question of leadership in general and ordin-ation in particular was passionately debated, with the result that there is now a deliberate effort to recognize a wide range of specialist ministers, such as youth specialists, evangelists, musicians and administrators. These ministers are not ordained into the ministry of word and sacrament, but they are ordained and they do belong to the national list of covenanted persons accredited for ministry.

BAPTIST LITURGY AND WORSHIP

Baptists are highly motivated and passionate about worship. Their services are usually participatory, and the styles of worship vary considerably according to the spirituality, theology and culture of the congregation. The majority of Baptist congregations are of a charismatic culture, and so the liturgy is prepared but free. A significant minority would seek to work within a more classical liturgical pattern but at the same time engaging enthusiastically with new forms of worship, such as Celtic and Taizé styles. The common characteristic across the board is that Baptists are not afraid of the new, and their worship delights in new forms and expressions.

BAPTIST CHURCH STRUCTURES

Baptist ecclesiology is rooted in the gathering together of the members of the local congregation. Membership and baptism are closely linked, as those who have been baptized commit themselves to living out their discipleship among a particular group of people. The church meeting is the place where those in membership meet together as an expression of their covenant commitment to one another, and it is the occasion when there is a shared process of discernment and decision-making. This is not a business meeting where only the loudest voices are heard or where a majority decision is sought; rather, it is a place where Christians listen to each other and to God through prayer and reflection, in order to discern the mind of Christ. For Baptists, membership of the Church universal is made real through membership of the local community.

The ministers and officers of a local church are elected by its members. Their authority is not automatically given by dint of their office, but rather grows through a process of trust-building and mutual relationships.

Beyond the local church, associations are now organised on a regional basis, with regional ministers forming association teams. Their task is to equip and resource the churches in pastoral and mission matters. Nationally the BUGB meets together annually in assembly, and between assemblies in an elected council. The national staff of the BUGB, led by a general secretary and senior management team, seek to serve and resource the constituent members of the BUGB: the churches, colleges and associations alike.

BAPTIST ECUMENICAL STRUCTURES

BUGB people are full members and active participants in the regional and national expressions of ecumenical life. Baptists have recently voted in assembly unanimously to endorse the resolution to continue as full members of CTBI and CTE. Baptists are deeply committed to ecumenical partnerships in mission at all levels of the church's life.

BAPTIST CHURCH LIFE, ETHOS AND CHARACTER

The profile and ethos of Baptist churches today is perhaps best described by those who see it from outside. Nevertheless, the indications are that the churches of the BUGB are in buoyant mood. Their passion for mission has never been stronger; the small but steady signs of growth are quietly encouraging. There is a collective commitment among the constituent parts of the BUGB to establish new and imaginative ways of being church in the twenty-first century. Practically speaking this means in worship there is a growing eclecticism drawing widely on contemporary, alternative, renewed, traditional and ancient traditions. In mission and evangelism there is a new, critical approach that discerns and distinguishes between good and bad practices. Baptists today, as at their beginning in the seventeenth century, remain radical evangelicals.

The Revd Myra Blyth
Assistant General Secretary, Baptist Union of Great Britain

BLACK MAJORITY CHURCHES

An encounter with the black majority churches within local ecumenical working would be one of diversity not homogeneity. Just as there are many different forms of church that originated in the Reformation, so there are different forms and emphases within black majority churches – there are African indigenous groups; Caribbean-originated churches, often strongly influenced by American Pentecostalism; and black British Pentecostal churches.

Of the Pentecostal black majority churches whose roots are traced from the US Pentecostal movement, from the Azusa Street movement in the 1920s, the largest is the 'Church of God' family within

Pentecostalism – the New Testament Church of God, the Church of God of Prophecy, and Apostolic churches. Their key statements of faith have a Trinitarian basis, with particular emphasis on the person and the work of the Holy Spirit evident in believers' lives as seen in the Bible in the Acts of the Apostles, Pauline letters (especially 1 Corinthians) and some parts of the Old Testament. An emphasis on Scripture is also important in the context of this part of the church family, informing a Christian way of living that shows as an identifying factor in a commitment to Christ, with a particular emphasis on holiness. The focus is on evangelism and mission, where looking forward to Christ's second coming undergirds the theology.

Many black majority churches bring together people who share a common heritage in a particular part of Africa, and they may include in their life and worship many of the cultural, spiritual and social traditions of, for example, Ghana or Nigeria. Some of these churches draw inspiration from a particular leader, who has had a prophetic ministry which has led a group of disciples out of one or more of the mainstream churches. The particular African cultural flavour of many of these churches is an aspect of the response to the gospel in the African context, during the post-colonial period, when churches wanted to move on from the patterns of Christianity that had been brought by missionaries from Europe and the USA. Sharing a building with black majority churches can prompt sometimes difficult conversations about inculturation, but it ought to help the white majority host-church to begin to examine the ways in which their own tradition represents the gospel inculturated into British society.

The spirituality of black majority churches draws on the tradition for worship shown in various psalms of praise in the book of Psalms. There is not usually a written liturgical form, but there is a pattern of lively and charismatic worship, with singing and prayer. Exhortation (encouragement and inspiration) and testimonies bring a personal dimension within the corporate aspect of the worshipping life of the congregation. Worship within the church setting is a vehicle to support devotional life and witness in the various contexts in which members of these congregations find themselves, relating the work of Christ to their wider communities. There is inspirational exposition of biblical text, usually by the pastor or leaders within the church, with an opportunity for a response or a short time of worship at the close, with prayer support from recognized members. Sunday worship may last for most of the day, and include eating together as well as worship, prayer and teaching.

The ministry of the church is primarily delivered through a pastor, who may be full time or may work and care for the congregation as well as going to a regular job. Lay people are also there as support in various roles in the areas of Christian education (preaching and teaching, prayer and evangelism) and counselling, children's and youth ministry, prison and hospital visits, care for the elderly and young – including the provision of supplementary education to support children within and outside the church who need extra help and nurseries. Pastoral care is delivered through home groups or requested visits from the church leadership team, which is important in supporting the preaching ministry within church life. The church is primarily self-financing and practises the discipline of tithing wherever possible. Many local churches are involved in community projects, which may be financed in partnership with local or central government.

There are different structures within the Pentecostal churches, which have autonomous leadership within the local context with identified lay or ordained leaders. Many leaders are theologically trained in universities, or in affiliated Bible schools within the church family structures that are university-accredited or recognized in Europe or the USA. Some, especially lay leaders, are recognized by various forms of commissioning within their local context and their call is usually identified by pastors or a combined executive board that is accountable to local, national or international headquarters. Local churches may be involved in various partnerships through councils of churches, such as the Council of African and African–Caribbean Churches, the International Ministerial Council of Great Britain, the Cherubim and Seraphim Council of Churches, the New Testament Assembly or the African and Caribbean Evangelical Alliance. Many local black majority congregations participate in national ecumenical instruments through affiliation to one of these councils. For some, their denominational allegiances will bring them together with other congregations to provide for the responsibilities of oversight and collective responses, and there may be local bishops or overseers, pastors, evangelists, deacons, elders, prophets, apostles and ministers, all of whom have leadership responsibilities.

The life of the church is congregationally based, and built around Sunday services, with midweek activities that support the church's ministry to its community with a cultural flavour from an African–Caribbean or African perspective, although some churches are increasingly multicultural in make-up. The local church's mission is not really geographically defined, with the congregation scattered over a wide area, and often travelling long distances to worship; black majority churches usually take seriously the great commission to go into all the world, and will minister across local borough and county boundaries. Conventions or convocations are key occasions for coming together, and are times of renewal, rededication and focus in the Pentecostal churches. They are held especially at Easter and in August, though this varies and some can be held at other times of the year. If you are seeking to work ecumenically with black majority churches, it is important to find out when this significant occasion is happening in the black Christian community calendar, and to go and participate, and enjoy the atmosphere and teaching. Conventions are usually local or regional but there are also national conventions for the larger denominational groupings of the black majority churches.

It has not always been easy for black majority churches to participate in working for unity in Britain. For many members there may be painful recollections of the rejection they experienced from the existing churches when they first arrived – churches which, for many of them, had been their home in the countries from which they came. For new generations, these memories of rejection are still around, and the black majority churches have developed a dynamic and evangelical life that may find the traditional agenda of English ecumenism irrelevant. However, some black majority churches are involved in working for unity, engaging locally in town-wide ecumenical initiatives for mission and evangelism, praying with partner churches, preaching and leading acts of worship, and engaging nationally in CTE and CTBI.

Many black majority churches share the buildings of other congregations, and these relationships vary from 'landlord and tenant'-type arrangements, where the two congregations barely know one another, to powerful expressions of an ecumenism that is about breaking down more than inter-church barriers. If your church is part of such an arrangement, it is important that you find ways to get to know your partner congregation, and perhaps to share in some mission or social activity together. Even if you have no formal sharing agreement, a hospitality agreement – which sets out what each party expects of the other – can be helpful in avoiding difficulties over those practical matters that are often a cause of trouble between churches sharing a building. Churches Together in England has produced a helpful leaflet – *Sharers, Guests or Tenants? The Sharing of Church Buildings in the Multicultural City* – which offers useful advice for those entering such an arrangement.

In developing ecumenical relations with black majority churches, there is no substitute for visiting local congregations for worship; the best sources of information can be found from local churches first-hand, especially through personal visits including a discussion with pastors.

Dean Pusey
Black Christian Concerns Group
Ecumenical Liaison Officer, CTBI

THE CHURCH OF ENGLAND

The Church of England is continuous with the Celtic and early Roman Churches in Britain. Some of its episcopal sees derive from this period. It affirms the ecumenical creeds of the early Church and continues the threefold ministry of bishops, priests (presbyters) and deacons from patristic times. But the Church of England has also been shaped in important ways by the Reformation. It affirms the centrality of Scripture (made available to the people in their own language), justification by grace through faith and the sharing of all baptized believers in the royal priesthood of Christ. Its ordained ministers are free to marry and it ordains women as deacons and priests (though not, at present, as bishops). The Church of England is thus both catholic and reformed.

At the same time, the Church of England (like Anglicanism generally) has been deeply influenced by the intellectual currents of modernity. It has been hospitable, after a struggle, to the contributions of the Renaissance, the Reformation, the Enlightenment, the scientific revolution and the various human and social sciences. It is responsive to cultural trends in the arts, especially literature. It is, on the whole, a tolerant church, willing to give fairly generous scope to theological exploration in dialogue with non-theological academic disciplines.

Its 'historic formularies' (the Thirty-nine Articles of Religion, the Book of Common Prayer, 1662, and the Ordering of Bishops, Priests and Deacons), which derive from the sixteenth and seventeenth centuries, are regarded as an 'inheritance of faith', sources of inspiration and guidance, especially for the clergy. There is an acknowledgement that the faith of the Church, as the Church of England has received it, needs to be expressed afresh in each generation. The historic formularies are, of course, subordinate in authority to the Bible and the creeds; and in fact help to interpret Scripture and the witness of the early Church. The formularies are complemented by the canons (decrees or laws), which include some important ecclesiological material, including much that is relevant to ecumenism.

The Church of England is part of the worldwide Anglican Communion of thirty-eight self-governing churches (many of them provinces). Its nearest Anglican neighbours are the Church in Wales, the Scottish Episcopal Church and the Church of Ireland. The churches of the Anglican Communion are 'in communion' with the Archbishop of Canterbury, who has a recognized ministry of pastoral leadership throughout the Communion. He invites the bishops of the Communion to the Lambeth Conference, in England, every ten years. The Lambeth Conference cannot take decisions that are binding on the member churches, but its resolutions and teachings have considerable moral authority.

The Church of England is also in communion with several other families of churches: most Nordic and Baltic Lutheran Churches (through the Porvoo Agreement of 1996), the Old Catholic Churches of the continent of Europe (through the Bonn Agreement of 1930–1), the Mar Thoma Church of India, the Philippine Independent Church and two small churches of the Iberian peninsula. An important litmus test of being 'in communion' is the interchangeability of episcopally ordained ministers.

However, the Church of England has recently entered into agreements that fall short of this, with other churches: the German Evangelical Church (EKD, through the Meissen Agreement), the Moravian Church in England (through the Fetter Lane Agreement) and the French Lutheran and Reformed Churches (through the Reuilly Agreement). These relationships are premised on agreement in the apostolic faith and on the goal of full visible unity. They involve mutual acknowledgement of one another as churches and a commitment to work towards ecclesial communion including the interchangeability of ministries. But this depends on agreement, which has not yet been attained in these cases, on the theology and practice of episcopal oversight, including ordination.

A variant of this approach is the proposals of the Formal Conversations (1999–2001) between the Church of England and the Methodist Church of Great Britain. Since there is agreement in principle between the two churches on episcopal oversight, the

Conversations envisage a national covenant that would provide an immediate springboard for the next stage towards organic unity.

The Church of England ordains bishops, priests and deacons in conformity with the practice of the primitive Church. Holy Order is seen as single and as threefold. The ordained are seen as representing both Christ and his body the Church in their ministry of word, sacrament and pastoral care. In that respect, Holy Order is sometimes said to be a sacramental sign of Christ's presence and work in and through the Church. Ordination is sequential so that one is always ordained to the diaconate first and the presbyterate next. A person ordained to any order can never lose the character of that order, so that the distinctive nature of the diaconate is carried into the presbyterate and that of each of these into the episcopate. The Church of England also has within its ministry those who remain in a 'renewed' or distinctive diaconate.

The Church of England strongly affirms the ministry of lay people. The laity play leading roles in the life and governance of the church at every level. Churchwardens and Readers are associated with the bishop in their particular forms of lay ministry. Lay ministries that are locally rather than nationally accredited include lay pastoral assistants and evangelists. Bishops have oversight of all aspects of accredited ministry, lay and ordained.

Worship in the Church of England has been conducted in the vernacular since 1549 and is liturgical, using a range of authorized forms from the Book of Common Prayer (1662) to *Common Worship* (2000). Anglican worship revolves around Morning and Evening Prayer (matins and evensong) and the Eucharist or Holy Communion. Other forms of service, such as family services, may be authorized by the bishop from time to time. Only priests and bishops may preside at the Eucharist, though deacons, Readers and others assist. Clergy, Readers and other assistants robe in cassock and surplice, especially for non-eucharistic services, and eucharistic vestments are widely used. In Anglican worship, words, music, colour, decoration, sacred imagery, movement (and sometimes incense) are all used to glorify God and uplift the worshipper. There is a balance and complementarity of word and sacrament, as befits a church that is both catholic and reformed.

As an 'established church', the Church of England is committed to a nationwide pastoral ministry, to full involvement in civil society and to making a contribution to the public discussion of issues that have moral and spiritual implications (at present twenty-six bishops sit in the House of Lords). This national ministry is carried out on a territorial basis, through the dioceses and the parochial system. The aim of this approach is to bring the ministry of the word, the sacraments and pastoral care within reach of all parishioners. This territorial method is complemented by extensive sector ministries (chaplaincies) on an institutional basis. The weakening of local attachments through social and economic mobility makes these sector ministries particularly important at the present time.

The 'occasional offices' are particularly important in the Church of England's pastoral mission in the community. Baptisms, marriages and funerals, as rites of passage, bring the clergy and those who assist them into contact with many parishioners who are not regular churchgoers. These pastoral contacts are valued by the church as opportunities for Christian instruction, for leading individuals towards a further stage of Christian initiation, or simply for building up an understanding and trust that may bear fruit in the future.

Confirmation is a rite of passage of a sacramental nature and is understood to be a means of grace within the process of Christian initiation and a source of strengthening by the Holy Spirit for Christian discipleship. The minister of confirmation is always the bishop as the 'chief pastor' of all within his diocese and 'their father in God'.

Shaped as it is by these rites of passage and by the Christian year with its liturgical seasons, festivals and penitential seasons, the ethos of Anglican spirituality is that of pilgrimage. It has an eschatological dimension – moving forward step by step in trustful discipleship into God's future. At the same time, Anglican spirituality is generally world-affirming and is comfortable with marriage, daily work, life in the community, participation in civil society and in political processes. Of course, Anglicans are sometimes slow to see the relevance of their faith to everyday life and struggle to reconcile spirit and body, the individual and the community, time and eternity. But the incarnational, sacramental spirit of Anglican spirituality is conducive to the integration of these.

Modern Anglicanism is both episcopal and synodical in its leadership and governance. It embodies the conciliar principles of constitutional authority, representation and consent. Lay people, clergy and bishops have particular responsibilities in the way that these principles are worked out at every level of the church's life.

Parochial church councils (PCCs) are the very local form of church government. Elected annually by all those baptized worshippers who enter their names on the parish electoral roll (this may include those who are also members of other churches), the PCC shares responsibility with the incumbent and churchwardens (the latter also being elected annually, but in theory by a wider parish constituency) for church life within the parish, including the church building, parish finances, worship and mission.

All parishes are represented by elected lay persons on the deanery synod, which has more of a reflective and supportive role and is not directly part of the legislative process of the Church of England. These deanery synod representatives form the electoral college for lay representatives on the diocesan and general synods. These are made up of houses of laity, clergy and bishops. Bishops have special but not exclusive responsibility for matters of faith and order, including ministry and worship. The House of Bishops consults together frequently on matters that are not confined to synodical business, and acts collegially.

New developments in the life of the church – such as the liturgical provisions of *Common Worship*, or the ordination of women to the priesthood – require two-thirds majorities in each of the houses voting separately. The General Synod is elected for a period of five years and is inaugurated in the presence of the Queen, who is the Supreme Governor (though without executive authority) of the established Church of England. It meets at least twice a year for a period of days. The two archbishops are its presidents but it is chaired by a panel that includes lay people. The General Synod includes ecumenical representatives who are non-voting members and welcomes guests from other partner churches.

The Church of England has contributed some outstanding leaders to the ecumenical movement: William Temple, George Bell, Oliver Tomkins. It has played a leading role in the Faith and Order Movement up to the present. Both the Lambeth Conference and the General Synod have consistently reaffirmed Anglican commitment to the ecumenical enterprise. As we have seen, the Church of England is assiduous in developing agreements with other churches with the intention of building on these in the future. The Ecumenical Canons (B43 and B44) set out a breadth of possibilities for local relationships and for Local Ecumenical Partnerships specifically.

However, the Church of England tends to fall between two stools when it comes to actually uniting with other churches. In theology and history it has much in common with the churches of the Reformation – who therefore tend to expect unity with Anglicans to be easier than it is. In church order it stands close to the Roman Catholic and Orthodox Churches – who therefore find it hard to understand Anglican doctrinal rapport with the Reformation tradition. The Church of England's track record shows it to be rather a risky partner in an ecumenical courtship.

The current ecumenical policy of the Church of England is realistic about these difficulties. It seeks to progress towards the ultimate goal of full visible unity by a series of agreed steps or stages so that issues can be dealt with sequentially and when, as sometimes happens, this proves difficult, the ground already gained is not lost. The Church of England is committed to all-round and every-level ecumenism. This ecumenical policy is primarily motivated not by pragmatism or sentiment but by a disciplined theological vision. The vision is shaped and encouraged by the foretaste of full visible unity that is granted to us in our experience of fellowship and collaboration in many areas of ecumenical life.

The Revd Prebendary Dr Paul Avis
General Secretary, Council for Christian Unity

THE CONGREGATIONAL FEDERATION

Congregationalism is a form of church order based on the local, gathered congregation. It arose in England and Wales in the sixteenth century as part of the European Reformation. Outlawed by refusal to conform to worship as laid down by the laws that established the Church of England, gatherings of nonconformist Christians worshipped in secret in houses, barns and in the open country, in danger of their lives. They took their stand on religious freedoms of congregations: to call their own elders, preachers and teachers; to worship without adherence to written forms of liturgy; and to order their own affairs. Not only 'Congregational' churches but Baptist, Independent Methodist and many Pentecostal churches are formed along congregational lines.

Congregational churches in Scotland arose in the context of the European Reformation but independently of the issues raised by the establishment of the Anglican Church in England and Wales.

The Congregational Federation was formed in 1972, from a substantial minority of congregations who wished to continue in the congregational tradition, when the majority of the then Congregational Church of England and Wales entered into organic union with the Presbyterian Church to form the United Reformed

Church. Some Scottish congregational churches have more recently joined the Federation.

THE LOCAL CONGREGATION

The foundation document of the Congregational Federation refers to 'the distinctive principle' of congregationalism, namely, 'the scriptural right of every separate church to maintain perfect independence in the government and administration of its own affairs'. This is a direct quotation from the foundation of the Congregational Union of England and Wales in 1831. The present Federation, like the former Union, 'shall not in any case assume legislative authority or become a court of appeal'.

Local churches guard their independence tenaciously. All decisions relating to the ordering of church life are taken by the church meeting; that is, the covenanted membership of the local church. Worshippers, after a period of continuous attendance determined by the church meeting, may apply for membership. If they are accepted by the church meeting, they are brought into membership, normally at a Communion service. Members generally meet monthly (or less often in the case of some smaller congregations). They may elect a committee of deacons, answerable to the church meeting, to serve the local church. This form of government means that decisions can be taken and enacted very quickly and the mission and life of the church can proceed at local level by the full involvement of the local people.

Each church has the authority to call and ordain its own minister. The fellowship of churches offers a scheme of training and recognition, and churches are encouraged to call ministers who have been trained and/or are recognized nationally, but this is by no means compulsory. This may, on occasion, lead to anomalous situations or to local churches making serious mistakes. On the other hand, it enables local churches to be open to the leading of the Holy Spirit and has led to empowering decisions. In the second decade of the twentieth century, it meant that congregationally ordered churches were the first to ordain women in Britain, Congregational churches ordaining their first woman in 1917. Since then, there has been a tradition of ordination being open to women as well as men. In the first instance, it was possible because training colleges could choose to offer training to women on the understanding that, if a local congregation chose to call a woman, no outside authority could gainsay it.

WORSHIP

Worship in Congregational churches is based on an oral tradition rather than on written liturgical resources. This does not mean that written resources are never used. Hymn books, for example, are widely used, and handbooks offer guidance for specific occasions such as weddings and funerals. However, where written resources are used, it is in the context of a fully oral tradition and they never have the status of authorized texts.

The order for worship is generally a balance of singing, Scripture-reading, prayer and preaching, with the sermon traditionally forming the climax of the service. While churches may choose to follow a lectionary or other seasonal pattern from time to time, most churches do not. Prayer and preaching are usually extempore or 'free'; that is, they are not written down, though they will usually have been prepared in outline. At its best, 'free' prayer and preaching draw on the solid scholarship and deep spirituality that have been the hallmark of congregational leadership.

Most Congregational churches share Communion, more often known as the Lord's Supper, once or twice a month. This is seen as a commemoration of the last supper shared by Jesus with his disciples and is done in obedience to his command to 'Do this in remembrance of me'. Traditionally, the table is open; that is, the invitation is to 'all who love the Lord Jesus Christ' to partake of the bread and wine. The congregation remains seated and deacons (elected by the church meeting) serve the bread and wine to people in their seats. Thus all eat the bread and drink the wine together in a corporate act, rather than in individual devotion.

MISSION AND UNITY

Congregationalists, like all the Christian denominations in Britain, engaged in world mission during the eighteenth and nineteenth centuries. The Council for World Mission was formed from the London Missionary Society, and serves Congregational, Presbyterian and some United/Uniting Churches. The Council was at the forefront of mission development in seeing missionary activity as the responsibility of local churches in every part of the world, supporting each other in partnership. True to the local emphasis of congregationalism, CWM sees the relationship between local churches as one of partnership and support rather than authority or dependency.

The Congregational Federation was a founder member of CTBI,

CTE and Cytun and has been active in the ecumenical life of Britain and Ireland. It has contributed to discussion of the ecumenical vision, advocating unity in diversity rather than older notions of organic union. Congregationalists remain enthusiastic supporters of churches working together, while retaining and enjoying their own distinctive identity.

The Revd Dr Janet Wootten
Minister at Union Chapel, London

THE EVANGELICAL ALLIANCE

The Evangelical Alliance is a membership body that unites a constituency of over 1 million Christians throughout the United Kingdom around the shared values of its Basis of Faith (Appendix 1) and within the framework of its Evangelical Relationships Commitment (Appendix 2).

In September 2000, after evaluation and review of this movement whose history goes back to 1846 but which enjoyed particular resurgence and visibility during the 1980s and 1990s, the vision of a 'movement for change – uniting to change society' was positively received by the membership.

The Evangelical Alliance has three categories of membership – personal, church (congregation) and organizational (including denominations). Over thirty denominations and streams of Christianity are organizational members. A wider range of churchmanship is represented through personal and church membership categories. Approximately 30 per cent of the membership is within the Anglican tradition.

The Evangelical Alliance operates in a threefold way:

- *resourcing* – largely through the resources of member societies;
- *networking* – on a geographical basis through local evangelical fellowships, or in subject areas, clustering member bodies who share a common concern;
- *voice* – functioning as a prophetic voice to society and a provocative voice to the Church.

Within the diverse membership of the Evangelical Alliance there is a variety of conviction and practice in terms of involvement in wider ecumenical structures. Clearly there are those who choose the Evangelical Alliance as an alternative arena for co-operative activity and fellowship; sometimes from conviction, sometimes for pragmatic reasons. Other members work very comfortably both with fellow evangelicals and in the wider ecumenical landscape.

Recent feedback from focus groups held around the United Kingdom suggested that the choice between involvement in a local evangelical grouping or a local Churches Together group is often based on the perceived effectiveness of the group in stimulating local mission or co-ordinating community activity. In other words, where a Churches Together group is perceived to be working effectively there may be less justification for the maintenance of a parallel evangelical grouping.

Operationally, Evangelical Alliance staff work widely within the broader framework of society and church, contributing for example to commissions of ecumenical bodies and working in a co-operative and co-belligerent manner on specific issues with community and campaigning groups. Senior staff liaise with their counterparts in the ecumenical bodies on a periodic basis.

Revd John S. Smith
UK Director, Evangelical Alliance

THE LUTHERAN COUNCIL OF GREAT BRITAIN

Lutherans have worshipped in England for centuries, though rarely in English until about forty years ago. The first official congregation was established in London in 1669, used by Germans and Scandinavians. By the end of the seventeenth century, two further congregations (one German and one Scandinavian) had been established. Now there are Lutheran parishes and congregations in all parts of the country and Lutheran worship is conducted in a wide range of languages in Britain, reflecting Lutheranism's international character – Amharic, Cantonese, Danish, English, Eritrean (Tigrinya), Estonian, Finnish, German, Hungarian, Icelandic, Latvian, Lithuanian, Mandarin, Norwegian, Polish, Swahili and Swedish. Together the various Lutheran churches in Britain minister to some 90,000 persons, mainly in languages other than English.

Lutherans profess the historic creeds of the Church, which proclaim that God is a Trinity – the Creator, Saviour and Comforter. Lutherans especially emphasize that God offers his eternal love to humans as a gift – it is not something that they can earn by what they do. In Christ, God has shown us that he accepts us as we are, with our many failings. By placing our trust in this gracious promise of God, we are put right with God. Lutherans sum this up by professing that we are justified by grace, through faith. Such faith empowers people to express love to their neighbours freely – not in an effort to win God's salvation, but in praise of the God who loves us unconditionally and eternally.

What Lutheran churches everywhere believe and profess is explained in detail in several confessional writings dating from the sixteenth century. The most fundamental of these is the Augsburg Confession. Throughout the world, the identity of Lutherans is closely linked to what they believe and proclaim rather than to particular styles or forms in church life.

As Lutheran services have been developed over the centuries in many different cultures and countries, there are inevitably variations in expressions and styles of worship, which are reflected in Lutheran worship in Britain. Generally, Lutheran services are in the 'catholic' tradition, following the ancient liturgies and observing historic usage. Some congregations, however, offer a simpler style of worship. Crucifixes, candles and religious art are common. In many Lutheran churches the priests or pastors wear traditional vestments, such as albs, stoles and chasubles. In other churches a black robe and ruff or bands are worn, often with a pectoral cross. Church buildings can be very ornate or rather simple, but always with the altar, pulpit and font as the main features. Differences in worship style or dress do not imply differences in theology or belief for Lutherans; often they have arisen for reasons of history or culture.

Martin Luther extolled music as a 'precious gift of God', and said that music had been bestowed on humanity 'to remind them that they are created to praise and magnify the Lord'. Certainly from Luther's time onwards, music has always been an important part of Lutheran worship. The liturgies are often sung by the clergy and the congregation – it can happen that the sermon is virtually the only part of the service that is not sung. Hymns and instrumental music are common. Many traditional Lutheran hymns are unfamiliar (and might seem a bit heavy) to most Christians in Britain, while others have entered the mainstream of British hymnody. Many of the older hymns are very long and strongly didactic, as they aimed at both beautifying the worship and instructing the congregation.

The musical aspect of Lutheran spirituality has given rise to much church music within Lutheranism. There have been many great Lutheran composers who wrote prolifically for their churches, such as Bach and Mendelssohn, and they still feature strongly in much Lutheran worship today.

The proclamation of the word is fundamental in Lutheran worship. It is 'evangelical' in the sense that the gospel of Christ is at the centre of all proclamation, presented as God's gift of grace for us. For Lutherans 'evangelical' does not describe a type of churchmanship or piety or polity, but the promise-character of the word, which should be at the heart of all proclamation. All Lutherans would call themselves 'evangelical' in this sense, and it sometimes surprises other Christians to discover that these 'evangelicals' might wear ornate vestments, use incense and refer to Holy Communion as 'the Mass'.

'Evangelical' proclamation happens, or should happen, in all aspects of Lutheran worship – hymns, liturgy, readings, sermons (which, in some cultures, are expected to be long and weighty) and in the celebration of the sacraments. Lutherans celebrate Holy Communion regularly, believing that Christ is really present in his fullness in the bread and wine of the sacrament, giving himself in his body and blood for the forgiveness of sins and spiritual nourishment. Usually communicants receive the wine from a common chalice, though in recent years individual cups have been used in some places. The bread is usually in wafer form and is put into the hand or placed into the communicant's mouth. Lutherans administer baptism to infants and adults, believing that God strengthens faith through the water used in this sacrament.

As with most other churches, Lutheran congregations and parishes in Britain have been influenced in recent decades by liturgical or spiritual renewal movements in their home churches. Generally, there is now greater lay involvement in worship, which traditionally had been led only by the pastor. The language of services has been updated, and musical settings and hymns offer many more styles and possibilities. There has also been a renewed interest in some older forms or practices that had been largely ignored, such as private confession, prayer candles, particular liturgies and pilgrimages.

There is no single pattern of organization among Lutheran churches, as no one particular structure is regarded by Lutherans as essential for the Christian Church. In considering how to organize themselves, Lutheran churches are free to be pragmatic. They may organize themselves in a range of ways to carry out their mission, adopting forms that suit their particular historical and cultural circumstances.

Some Lutheran churches have maintained the 'historic episcopacy' (an unbroken chain of bishops from the early days of the Church);

others have not. Although many have bishops or archbishops as their senior pastors and administrators, others elect presidents, who may be lay people, for set terms of office. In some churches the local congregation has a very strong voice; in others the central church has great authority. Most Lutherans have synods or church assemblies that play an important role in the election of bishops and other church leaders, and in approving church policies and programmes.

On the global level, the Lutheran Church has been engaged in productive discussions for many years with the Roman Catholic Church, which have helped the two churches to deepen their understanding and appreciation of each other. On 31 October 1999 the Vatican and the Lutheran World Federation signed a historic agreement that confirms their shared understanding of the doctrine of justification, which had been a major stumbling block on the road to unity since the sixteenth century.

In recent years Nordic and Baltic Lutheran churches have entered into a new relationship with the Anglican churches of Britain and Ireland, which includes intercommunion and the exchange of priests. Lutheran and Anglican churches in certain other parts of the world (such as Canada and the USA) have also established intercommunion. In some countries Lutheran churches and Reformed churches have close relations, including intercommunion and ministerial exchange. Through these relationships and in many other ways Lutherans strive for reconciled diversity in the one body of Christ.

Established in 1948, the Lutheran Council of Great Britain represents and co-ordinates the common work of eleven different Lutheran churches that have congregations or chaplaincies in Great Britain.

The Revd Thomas Bruch
Lutheran Council of Great Britain

THE METHODIST CHURCH

The Methodist Church is the fourth largest church in Britain after the Anglican and Roman Catholic Churches and the Church of Scotland. It is a community of just over a million people in England, Scotland and Wales. Of these over 300,000 are recorded as active members in about 6,000 local churches. These churches are the primary focus for worship Sunday by Sunday. Most of them are small (with fewer than fifty members) and very many are rural.

The churches are grouped into 600 or so circuits, which are the primary unit for mission and ministry. In each circuit one minister is the superintendent, responsible for upholding the discipline and decisions of the Methodist Conference, the governing body of the Methodist Church. He or she leads a ministry team, which will often include other ministers, deacons and lay people exercising specific ministries. These include nearly 10,000 local preachers, who are trained lay people accredited to lead worship and preach in their own circuit. They conduct the majority of Sunday services in Methodist churches.

The circuits are grouped together in 33 districts (including three in Wales, two in Scotland and one each in the Channel Islands and the Isle of Man); each with a minister who is appointed to chair the District Synod. The wider role of this minister is defined as 'furthering the work of God in the District' and there is a specific responsibility of oversight and pastoral care towards ministers and leadership of all the people in the district.

This whole network of churches, circuits and districts linked with the Conference is described as the 'connexion', an eighteenth-century word Methodists still use. It expresses interdependence and mutual support and can be a focus for vision. Having a connexional rather than a congregational structure means that the whole church acts and decides together and the local church never stands alone.

That word 'connexion' is a reminder of Methodist history. In May 1738 John Wesley and his brother Charles, priests of the Church of England, both underwent a profound spiritual experience. John described this in his journal for 24 May 1738:

> In the evening I went very unwillingly to a society in Aldersgate Street, where one was reading Luther's preface to the Epistle to the Romans. About a quarter before nine, while he was describing the change which God works in the heart through faith in Christ, I felt my heart strangely warmed. I felt I did trust in Christ, Christ alone, for salvation, and an assurance was given me that he had taken away my sins, even mine and saved me from the law of sin and death.

From that point John Wesley had a hugely influential preaching ministry. He also had a flair for organization. Wherever he went he formed societies made up of small groups, called 'classes', each with a lay leader, encouraging the members to grow in holiness, seeking 'perfect love'. After Wesley's death in 1791 the new movement became a separate church.

Since then there have been huge changes in the relationship of Methodism to other Christian traditions, its place in British society and its local expression in different parts of Britain and around the world. By the end of the nineteenth century there had been a number of splits and most of the branches of Methodism saw themselves as Free Churches, identifying themselves with the emerging nonconformist conscience.

After the union in 1932 of the Primitive, United and Wesleyan Methodist Churches, the Methodist Church was involved in the liturgical, theological and ecumenical changes and movements that have affected the life of most of the mainstream churches.

The 1932 Deed of Union set out the doctrinal standards of the Methodist Church. It insists on the primacy of Scripture, brought to life and interpreted by the Holy Spirit, in shaping and expressing faith and affirms that the original connexion of religious societies had become a church:

> The Methodist Church claims and cherishes its place in the Holy Catholic Church which is the Body of Christ. It rejoices in the inheritance of the apostolic faith and loyally accepts the fundamental principles of the historic creeds and of the Protestant Reformation. It ever remembers that in the providence of God Methodism was raised up to spread scriptural holiness through the land by the proclamation of the evangelical faith and declares its unfaltering resolve to be true to its divinely appointed mission.

Methodism has a strong sense of its place in the world Church. Every member of the Methodist Church is a member of the Methodist Missionary Society. Today almost all the churches that began life because of British Methodist missionary work are either part of united churches or autonomous Methodist Churches. There are also United Methodist Churches worldwide that are part of the American Methodist tradition.

The British Methodist Church plays its part in the World Methodist Council, made up of seventy churches from 108 countries. They vary greatly in their polity and practice and the Council, which meets every five years, is consultative and co-operative rather than legislative. It has been the vehicle for international dialogues with the Roman Catholic Church and Lutheran, Reformed and Anglican world bodies.

Within its understanding of the varied ministries of the whole people of God, the Methodist Church recognizes two orders of ordained ministry: the diaconate and the presbyterate. The diaconate is not only an order of ministry but a religious order with a rule of life. Deacons are a focus for the servant ministry of Christ and the Church. Those who are to be ordained as presbyters are not ordained to the diaconate first. They are known as 'ministers' and have a ministry of word and sacrament and pastoral oversight. They represent both Christ and the people of God, focusing in their ministry the ministry entrusted by Christ to the Church as his body.

The Methodist Church recognizes the importance of pastoral oversight (*episkope*). The oversight of the Conference is expressed, by delegation, both personally and through the councils of the church. A good example of how this works is in the ordering of Sunday worship. The Conference authorizes orders of service and has oversight of the training of those who lead worship. The *Methodist Worship Book* (1999) offers services that will stand the test of time, bear frequent repetition and provide a norm and a standard. Locally the superintendent minister and local preachers' meeting are responsible for the way services are conducted, whether using fixed forms or freer expressions of worship.

Methodist spirituality is hugely varied. It deliberately holds together dimensions that are often kept apart. It is both inward and outward, personal and corporate. It is about love for God and love for people. It embraces the ministry of the word and the ministry of the sacraments, liturgical prayer and the prayer of the heart, social concern and a sense of heaven. Distinctively Methodist resources include Charles Wesley's hymns, the Covenant Service, sharing in small groups, connexional networking, and commitment to both evangelism and dialogue. But Methodists find spiritual sustenance from many sources, probably even wider than those from many traditions with which their founder nurtured the early Methodists.

The Methodist Church believes its calling is to respond to the gospel of God's love in Christ and to live out its discipleship in worship and mission. Within that it has a vision of one Church for one world, a desire to share in a common life with all Christian people and a commitment to seeking the full visible unity of the Church. This is expressed through relationships with partner churches worldwide, the sharing of resources and giving and receiving in mission.

Much ecumenism begins with personal friendships but, for the sake of order and continuity, relationships and partnerships are expressed in formal, structured ways. So Methodism is involved in over 700 Local Ecumenical Partnerships in England and plays a full part in the ecumenical instruments in Britain and beyond.

Within the common search for Christian unity, relations between Anglicans and Methodists have been particularly close. The two churches have a shared commitment to seeking the visible unity of the Church locally, nationally and worldwide. This is affirmed when we declare in the Creed our shared belief in the one, holy, catholic and apostolic Church. In all ecumenical conversations the Methodist Church recognises a threefold responsibility: to be faithful to its own tradition, to be willing to share it with others and to be open to receive from others.

The Revd Peter Sulston
Co-ordinating Secretary for Inter-Church and Other Relationships,
Methodist Church

THE MORAVIAN CHURCH

What's in a name? To be known as the Moravian Church is not always helpful and, especially during the First and Second World Wars, the name was a source of suspicion. In fact, the formal name is the 'Unitas Fratrum' and the title 'Moravian Church' is simply a popular name used in the English-speaking world for the 'Unity of the Brethren'. The name arose because it was the migration of refugees from Moravia to Herrnhut in Saxony that led to the Renewed Moravian Church emerging from Herrnhut in the 1720s. The Unitas Fratrum (commonly known as the Ancient Unity) dates from 1957.

The Moravian Church in Great Britain and Ireland is one of the nineteen provinces worldwide that make up the Moravian Unity. In addition to Great Britain, the Moravian Church is to be found in the USA, Canada, Labrador and Alaska; the Caribbean, Central America, Suriname and Guyana; South Africa, Tanzania and reaching out into the surrounding countries; Northern India, Assam and Nepal as well as mainland Europe. As with other international communions, the fastest growing areas of the church are in Africa and the majority of Moravians are to be found there too.

The ultimate governing body is the Unity Synod which meets every seven years and comprises representatives from each of the nineteen provinces as well as from theological institutions and other Unity undertakings. The constitution of the Unity is the Church Order of the Unitas Fratrum (COUF). Within this framework, each province is autonomous and has its own church order which may not conflict with COUF. Each province is governed by its provincial synod. In Great Britain, Synod is convened every two years.

So, what of the Moravian Church in Britain and Ireland today? We have an extremely small presence here with only thirty-five congregations – five in Northern Ireland, five in Lancashire, six in Yorkshire, five in the Midlands, seven in the West and seven in London and the home counties. The majority of these congregations were settled in the middle and late eighteenth century in places where the Moravians were invited to preach.

At that time, the main focus of the church was mission and maintenance was not a priority. This approach, coupled with a reluctance to be seen in competition with other churches, especially the established church, has meant that although there were at one time hundreds of preaching places around the county, very few of these groupings ever became settled congregations.

In Germany, homeland of the renewed Moravian Church, Moravians lived in settlements that were self-sustaining communities. Members lived in 'choir' houses according to their age and marital status. For example, single women lived in the 'Sisters' House', single men in the 'Brethren's House', widows in their house, etc. Everyone was expected to make an economic contribution to the community and many cottage industries were set up.

This pattern was also followed in some areas in Britain and Ireland, with settlement buildings still to be found in Gracehill in Northern Ireland, Fairfield in Manchester, Fulneck near Leeds and Ockbrook near Derby. These are now communities where members can live in close proximity to their church.

The Moravian Church has always placed great emphasis on education and has run schools alongside its churches. In the UK most of the schools were absorbed into the state system when it was set up but it does still have two independent boarding schools – one at Ockbrook and the other at Fulneck – in the heart of the settlements.

One of the important aspects of recent years has been the injection of new life into the church received through the immigration of Moravian brothers and sisters from the Caribbean in the 1950s and 1960s. The British province benefited from this influx of members and now in Birmingham, Leicester and London the vast majority of Moravians are of Afro-Caribbean descent.

So, today we have tiny village congregations, lively city congregations and traditional congregations. Four congregations are united with the United Reformed Church, one worships in Methodist premises and one in a parish church. We have men as well as women ministers, paid and unpaid.

The Moravian Church has maintained a threefold order of ministry since 1467 when the first synod took place at Lhotka in Bohemia. Following ordination as a deacon, all sacramental roles may be exercised and consecration as a presbyter does not confer any additional authority – it is normally seen as the church's affirmation of a deacon's ministry. Bishops are elected by synod from among the presbyters and exercise a pastoral role. They are consecrated bishops of the whole Unity and not of any particular province.

Worship styles vary greatly between congregations and reflect the occasion as well as the composition and temperament of the congregation. There are a number of set orders of service that may be used if wished. The Moravian hymnbook contains a number of hymns by Moravian hymnwriters as well as many widely known hymns. The Moravian Church practises either infant or adult baptism and, as this marks admission into the Christian Church, baptisms normally take place during a normal worship service.

Count Zinzendorf, the most influential of the early leaders of the Renewed Moravian Church, did not envisage his work as becoming a separate denomination. His intention was to work with small groupings within existing churches, who would then strengthen and enthuse the whole body. As with Wesley, a contemporary of Zinzendorf, this ideal could not be put into practice and both men found that they had to set up independent bodies.

With this background, it is therefore only to be expected that the Moravian Church is ecumenical in outlook and practice, belonging to the national ecumenical bodies and having signed a declaration pledging mutual working and sharing where possible with the churches of England and Ireland. Congregations are expected to work ecumenically at the local level in whatever ways present themselves.

Mrs Jackie Morten
Member of the Provincial Board of the Moravian Church

THE ORTHODOX CHURCH

The Orthodox Church traces its roots to apostolic times, and its teachings have been largely formulated and confirmed by the ecumenical councils that took place in the Christian East during the first millennium. There has been no comparable council since 787, although plans are afoot for the convocation of another. Since Byzantine

emperors were the convenors of such councils, the absence of a comparable figure in our times creates several problems of precedence
and procedure.

Even this betrays a certain bias towards medieval ways of ordering church life. But this is considered a virtue. Tradition is revered,
and there is no period of Orthodox church history that could be
designated in Western terms as a reformation.

The Creed of Nicaea-Constantinople is universally accepted as
an index to the teaching of the Church. But this creed has never
included the phrase *Filioque* ('and the Son') to describe the proces-
sion of the Holy Spirit. This was added by Western Christians by the
end of the first millennium, and the Orthodox deny its validity to
this day.

The church is Trinitarian in its faith. The incarnation of God's
Son brings about the salvation of humankind, which people are
encouraged to achieve by means of co-operation or synergy with
their Saviour. There is no doubt that a fall necessitated such salvation. But the fall is not believed to have had an ineradicable effect
on humankind's potential. The richness of that potential is demonstrated in the lives of saints, first of whom is Mary, the Birthgiver of
God (her title since 449).

THE CHURCH THROUGHOUT THE WORLD

The church is one, and the use of the phrase 'Orthodox churches'
refers (awkwardly) merely to the separate bodies which exist within
it. These do not have an immutable character. Historical circumstances gave birth to a Greek Orthodox Church, and only in the early
nineteenth century. Almost as young are the present-day Bulgarian
and Romanian Churches. Even the Russian Orthodox Church has
had little more than a thousand years of existence. By contrast, the
patriarchates of Constantinople, Antioch and Alexandria stretch
back to the late Roman Empire. These are all independent or 'auto-
cephalous'. Hence the need for yet another universal council to
promote a corporate reassessment of their inner and their outer life.
That they have not deviated from each other in essentials over centuries of separation is a cause for wonder.

ORTHODOX WORSHIP

Byzantine ways of worship have predominated in the Orthodox
world, and this despite the various cultural backgrounds of the
individual churches. The annual and seasonal cycles of the services

are complex. And although the services often anticipate the worshippers' participation (many involve a dialogue between the clergy and the people), that very complexity, as well as the abstruseness of the language often used, tend to restrict oral involvement to the well-versed few. This has the virtue of encouraging the silent, and by no means passive, involvement of the many. Most of the services are sung as well as chanted. The melodies or (where used) the harmonies tend to reflect the local culture. The normal position for prayer is upright. Such is also the position for Communion.

Communion is restricted to the faithful, and intercommunion is discouraged even in mixed-marriage situations. Furthermore, Communion is often treated as an awesome, hence a rare, event. It thus requires due preparation.

Worship necessarily involves a spiritual commitment. Nonetheless, the use of all the senses is encouraged. Oral, aural, tactile, olfactory and visual factors all play their part. It is not unusual for an icon to be censed and kissed while an appropriate hymn is chanted.

ORTHODOX SPIRITUALITY

The normal liturgical and sacramental round of church life presupposes and nourishes the spirituality of the faithful. At the same time, the Orthodox Church has a rich tradition of individual prayer. There is a framework of daily devotions, which most people will adapt to their own circumstances and requirements. There is also the more dedicated and demanding practice of continuous prayer, centred on the invocation of the name of Jesus. This has developed since early times in monastic circles, but has much wider relevance and application.

Monasticism has played a prominent part in Orthodox church life since this form of dedication first developed. England has few monasteries (the most notable of which is to be found at Tolleshunt Knights in Essex). But the monastic spirit manifests itself in every diocese since bishops may be chosen only from the monks.

ORTHODOX MINISTRY

There is a threefold ministry of bishops, priests and deacons. Properly speaking, there should be a single bishop in a given diocese. In actual fact, the disparate sources of the Orthodox diaspora in England (for such it was and, for the most part, still remains) determines that different church authorities appoint or validate their separate bishops. In every case, the ultimate authority is vested in some distant patriarchate (Constantinople, Moscow, Belgrade-Pec). No mechanism for regular consultation of all the bishops resident or active in these islands has been instituted yet.

ORTHODOX CHURCH LIFE

Not only have the Orthodox arrived in England as immigrants; many seek to safeguard their Orthodoxy by keeping to their parental languages and customs. This determines the language of worship. It also helps to determine the language of parish social life. Not that assimilation does not make its inroads. Equally important in bringing the English language into play is the vigorous minority of British converts to the faith. There are thus a number of parishes where English is the dominant language, or even the only one.

ORTHODOX ECUMENICAL OUTLOOK

The Orthodox Church has played an important part in the initiation and development of the ecumenical movement. Indeed, a London-based bishop of the Constantinople patriarchate was one of the founder presidents of the World Council of Churches (1948). Previously, that same patriarchate had issued a notable appeal for ecumenical endeavour which was rare for its time (1920). In due course, and until recent times, most Orthodox churches were to work along such lines. In Britain, several of the local Orthodox churches belonged to BCC, and subsequently to CCBI and CTBI. These same churches have also been members of CTE.

Such participation is not enough to determine the attitude of each and every community, where immigrant insularity tends to confirm a traditionalist concern for the primacy and integrity of Orthodox values, and to discourage open-hearted collaboration with other Christian bodies.

The Very Revd Dr Sergei Hackel
Archpriest, Russian Orthodox Church

ORIENTAL ORTHODOX CHURCHES

The Oriental Orthodox Churches are (in alphabetical order) the Armenian, Coptic, Eritrean, Ethiopian, Syrian and Syro-Indian Orthodox Churches.

HISTORICAL INTRODUCTION

The family of Orthodox Apostolic Churches traces its origin to the cradle of Christianity. The first communities that the apostles formed were in Jerusalem, Alexandria (the see of St Mark), Antioch (the first see of St Peter) where 'the disciples were first called "Christians"' (Acts 11:26), and also in India, the land of the mission of St Thomas.

Although our churches have never really possessed worldly power, as Jesus said, 'My kingdom is not of this world', they were the beacons of the Christian mission during the early centuries of the rise and spread of Christianity, when their missionaries reached out into Asia and Africa. They accepted and still believe in conclusions of the first three ecumenical councils: Nicaea (325), Constantinople (381) and Ephesus (431). Because of cross-cultural misunderstandings and the power politics at play at the time, the Oriental Orthodox Churches were denied the right to attend and fully participate in the sessions of the Council of Chalcedon (451). It has to be said in Christian spirit that the Council of Chalcedon was neither inclusive nor a platform of ecclesiastical free debate for Christian unity. Consequently, the Oriental Orthodox family could not ratify its resolutions; moreover, they refused the *Tome of Leo*. Ever since they have been, inaccurately, known as non-Chalcedonian Orthodox, marginalized, persecuted and designated as Monophysites. No well-informed ecumenist, theologian or academic from the Chalcedonian world today would feel comfortable with this terminology. These misnomers will not hold the tide of Christian unity in fulfilment of our Lord's passion for unity. 'Let them be one'.

The Oriental Orthodox suffered immeasurably as they were dispersed far and wide. Their determination and consolation were derived from our Lord's promise, 'It is through many persecutions that we must enter the kingdom of God' (Acts 14.22). The diaspora brings its mixed blessings to the lives, witness and growth of our churches. The extent of the Oriental Orthodox diaspora today is surprising.

ORIENTAL ORTHODOX DOGMA AND TRADITION

Oriental Orthodox Churches are apostolic churches of the word and the sacrament. The Holy Bible (Old and New Testament) is the Alpha and Omega of their teaching and mission. The sacraments are central to our life, worship and spirituality. Our churches believe in seven sacraments: baptism, confirmation, penance, Holy Eucharist, matrimony, Holy Orders and orders for the sick (or extreme unction).

Liturgies were written especially to celebrate each sacrament and for other ecclesiastical events and feasts. The Holy Eucharist has been celebrated in our churches since the Last Supper, as instructed by our Lord 'Do this in remembrance of me' (Luke 22.19). In the main we use the ancient Sacred Liturgy of St James, who was the brother of our Lord and the first Bishop of Jerusalem. This was written in Aramaic, which was spoken in Galilee where Jesus taught. Syriac is still the liturgical language of some of our churches. Many other liturgies were developed and adopted from St James, which are currently in use in our churches today. The Nicene Creed is recited every time we celebrate the Holy Eucharist as a continual reminder of the pillars of our faith.

The Holy Trinity is central to our churches and teaching. Our churches pay special attention to the spiritual lives and practice of their faithful. This derives from the rich Christian spiritual heritage that developed in Palestine, Mesopotamia, Egypt and India. In addition to the Holy Bible, the sacrament and the sacred liturgies, our spiritual lives are continually nourished by the teaching, witness and martyrdom of the fathers of our churches. Church music, spiritual songs, fasting, celebrations of feasts and pilgrimages have their special uplifting functions. Finally, we were instructed to 'pray without ceasing' (1 Thessalonians 5.17) and prayer has a central role to play in our belief and spirituality.

ORIENTAL ORTHODOX ECCLESIASTICAL HIERARCHY AND AUTHORITY

The Oriental Orthodox Churches are centrally administered by the patriarchate and holy synods. The patriarch is the supreme head of the Church; he oversees the holy synods, which are the highest ecclesiastical and administrative authority, responsible for the smooth running of all church affairs. Archbishops and bishops report to the patriarchate, and are usually members of the holy synods. An archbishop or bishop is autonomous in his diocese. He presides over the diocese's council, which normally consists of lay men and women members. Pastoral care and other church duties are largely carried out by married priests and in some case by monks and nuns. Deacons carry out liturgical, pastoral and administrative duties in the diocese and parish.

- The Armenians' Apostolic Church is in Etchmiadzin, Armenia, under the jurisdiction of His Holiness Karekin II, Supreme Patriarch and Catholicos of all Armenians.
- The Coptic Orthodox Church is in Cairo, Egypt, under the jurisdiction of His Holiness Pope Shenouda III, Pope of Alexandria and Patriarch of the Coptic Orthodox Church.
- The Eritrean Orthodox Church is based in Asmara, Eritrea, under the jurisdiction of His Holiness Philippos I, Patriarch of the Eritrean Orthodox Church.
- The Ethiopian Orthodox Church is in Addis Ababa, Ethiopia, under the jurisdiction of His Holiness Abba Paulos, Patriarch of the Ethiopian Orthodox Tewahedo Church.
- The Syrian Orthodox Church of Antioch is in Damascus, Syria, under the jurisdiction of His Holiness Moran Mor Ignatius Zakka I. Iwas, Patriarch of Antioch and All the East and the Supreme Head of the Syrian Orthodox Church.
- The Syrian Orthodox Church of India, in Kerala, is administered by His Beatitude Mor Basilius, Catholicos of the Syrian Orthodox Church in India, under the jurisdiction of the Patriarch of Antioch and All the East.

ORIENTAL ORTHODOX ECUMENICAL PARTICIPATION

The Council of Oriental Orthodox Patriarchs meets regularly to decide on ecumenical policies and to encourage a dialogue with Orthodox, Catholic and Protestant Churches; it assesses their participation in international, regional and local ecumenical councils.

All the Oriental Orthodox Churches are members of the WCC and regional ecumenical councils. All the Oriental Orthodox Churches have dioceses and parishes in Britain and Ireland; some were established in the 1800s. They are headed either by a bishop or are under direct control of the patriarchate. They are represented by the Council of Oriental Orthodox Churches, which is a full member of CTBI and CTE, and participates in many of their commissions, fora and committees.

Aziz Nour
Secretary, Council of Oriental Orthodox Churches

THE RELIGIOUS SOCIETY OF FRIENDS (QUAKERS)

Quakers are convinced that every human being can have a direct and personal relationship with God, without need of any mediation, whether from clergy, liturgy or sacraments. It is our experience that by waiting on God in silent worship, we can come closer to God and learn better how God wants us to express our faith in action in our lives.

The Religious Society of Friends grew up in northern England in the religious turmoil of the seventeenth century. Early Friends wanted to revive the 'pure' Christianity of the early Church in the time of the apostles, before it got bogged down, as they perceived it, in structures and hierarchies. They were called 'Quakers' because they were said to quake in the presence of the Lord, and the name has stuck. Quakerism spread rapidly throughout England and to north America; missionary work in the twentieth century, mostly by north American Friends, caused it to spread worldwide.

Quakers in Britain meet in silence, waiting on the word of God for each one of us. It is our conviction that in the silence Christ is present; as George Fox the founder of the Quakers put it: 'Christ is come to teach his people himself'. Sometimes this knowledge comes as a personal experience within the heart, sometimes as a wider message that is conveyed to the whole meeting in spoken ministry. An hour's meeting might include four or five such contributions, or it might continue in silence for the whole period. There is no liturgical form to the Meeting for Worship, though two Friends appointed as elders will normally shake hands to indicate its end. Visitors are very welcome at all Quaker Meetings for Worship, and it is in the nature of the worship that any visitor can take a full part in the proceedings.

Quakers understand, and increasingly respect, the importance of the outward sacraments to most Christians. However, Friends would say that, for us, since membership of the true, invisible Church is known only to God, it cannot necessarily be conveyed by an outward human form, namely water baptism. Since we believe that Christ is present in a very real sense in our Meetings for Worship, we do not feel the need to celebrate the Eucharist as a particular outward form of that presence. Moreover, that aspect of the Eucharist which looks towards Christ's future coming in glory is at odds with our conviction that the kingdom of Christ is already present and can be known in this world. However, Friends have a strong sense of the sacramentality of the whole of life, that any and every part of life can be a vehicle for conveying the complete connection between the human and the divine.

Spoken prayer and readings from the Bible are less likely to form part of a Meeting for Worship, though they may well feature deeply in individual Friends' spiritual lives. Friends understand the Bible as a source of guidance rather than the once-and-for-all revealed word of God, and try to feel for the spirit in which it was originally written, the spirit which is present beneath the words. Creeds in particular are not used by Friends; we regard any such verbal formulae as fettering the free action of the Holy Spirit.

Quakers are firm believers in the priesthood of all believers; that empowered by the Holy Spirit individual church members with varieties of gifts are inspired and led into different varieties of service. British Quakers have no paid ministers, but appoint members of each meeting for a fixed period of service to undertake the range of necessary tasks. Each meeting has a clerk, who conducts the business meetings, which are also held in a spirit of worship; this will usually be the Friend who responds to correspondence on behalf of the meeting and can most appropriately represent it at ecumenical or other occasions. Meetings also appoint groups of overseers – who see to the pastoral relationships within the meeting – and elders, whose responsibility it is to help the meeting deepen its spiritual and corporate life.

Quakers meet both for worship and business in local groups, known as 'Preparative Meetings'. A group of these local meetings, roughly at county level, is organized into a regional or Monthly Meeting, and it is at this level that one's membership is held and much of the administration of the Society is carried out. At a national level, Quakers are organized in self-governing churches, known as 'Yearly Meetings'. Any Friend can attend a Yearly Meeting, which, as its name implies, meets annually as a decision-making body and which alone can take decisions on matters of significance to Friends throughout the country. Each meeting records its decisions in a minute, approved by those present, which embodies the sense of the meeting and carries the authority of the meeting. This way of organizing the visible church is very important to Friends. It provides a structure of local, regional and national meetings through which decisions can be made at an appropriate level. And all meetings, at whatever level, are conducted under the discipline of gathered waiting to discern the will of God and with the conviction that Christ will preside and lead the meeting into unity.

Service in and for the world is central to Friends' understanding of what God wants of us. From their earliest days Friends have tried to make their lives a testimony to the power of God in their own lives; particular aspects of this witness have been formulated over the years into distinctive individual and corporate testimonies, such as the peace testimony which informs Friends' work for non-violent resolution of conflict, and the testimonies to equality and simplicity, which increasingly inform our understanding of global and environmental issues. Friends are not always at one in the working out of these testimonies, and we have experienced internal conflict over moral stances taken by individuals and groups of members. But we are convinced that the indwelling Spirit of God calls us to a moral response to the struggles of humanity in the contemporary world and to working for its transformation.

Worldwide, there are about seventy self-governing Yearly Meetings; they are all represented on an international body, the Friends World Committee for Consultation. During the periods of rapid expansion in Quakerism – for example, in America in the nineteenth century – it was found more convenient to employ pastors and to adopted more programmed Meetings for Worship, more on the pattern of the evangelical churches. It is this 'programmed' form of Quakerism which, as a result of missionary activity, now forms the majority Quaker strand in Africa and Latin America, so the British form of 'unprogrammed' Quakerism now finds itself in a minority position among Quakers worldwide. This implies a considerable need for ecumenical activity within our own membership, which has only recently been recognized.

Friends in Britain have been involved in ecumenical activity throughout the last century, not only in the 'life and work' strand of this activity, but also in issues of faith and order. If membership of these bodies is defined by a credal formula, this poses difficulties for us, and hence we were associate members of the British Council of Churches, but the new ecumenical instruments set up in 1990 recognized Friends' testimony against creeds in an exemptive clause, which lays it upon the other members of these bodies to affirm that in their opinion, the Religious Society of Friends manifests faith in Christ in its life and work. We are deeply grateful for this recognition, and though individual Friends still have difficulty with our membership, the Yearly Meeting as a whole has embraced it warmly, and takes as full a part in ecumenical life, at local, regional and national level, as our distinctive practices allow. Since the World Council of Churches retains its credal membership formula, although Friends from more programmed Yearly Meetings are full members, Friends in Britain relate to the WCC through our own international body, Friends World Committee for Consultation.

Rowena Loverance
Religious Society of Friends

THE ROMAN CATHOLIC CHURCH

The Roman Catholic Church is a worldwide church and communion of local churches embracing many races and cultures. In the nineteen Roman Catholic dioceses in England the leadership of the church is exercised by the Catholic Bishops' Conference of England and Wales, in communion with the Bishop of Rome, and the church is committed to working with all Christians in mission and service to all people.

CHURCH

Roman Catholics understand the mystery of the Church as:

- present in every diocese (the local or particular church united with its bishop) and expressed and embodied in each congregation gathered to hear and proclaim the word of God and celebrate the Eucharist – the chief means by which the communion of the whole body is sustained and built up; and
- expressed also in the worldwide church which consists in and arises out of these local churches; the church is both universal in time and space, a spiritual community of all those throughout the ages united to the Trinity, and also a worldwide society structured with hierarchical organs, where unity is symbolized and sustained by communion with the see of Rome.

Roman Catholics believe that the Church is both a sign and an instrument of Christ's activity in the world. Although the Church is a very human institution, with all the limitations that belong to human institutions, we believe that Christ so identifies himself with the Church that it has a divine aspect and power that nothing can destroy.

God has created all human beings to a new life, and it is only by the death and resurrection of Christ that this is possible. Christ, the one and only Mediator, founded and ceaselessly sustains his Church as a visible society that gives grace and truth to all. The Spirit, sent at Pentecost, makes the Church holy, so that all believers can come to the Father through Christ, in the Spirit.

ROMAN CATHOLIC AUTHORITY

In Roman Catholic belief a key part in handing on Christ's message was shared by him with the apostles, chosen by Christ and eventually led by Peter. Others who continued their work of leadership in pastoral care, teaching and worship succeeded the apostles. These successors became known as 'bishops' under the leadership of the Bishop of Rome, whom Roman Catholics regard as the successor of Peter. Bishops share some of their authority with priests and deacons. The apostles entrusted the faith contained in sacred Scripture and tradition to the whole church, and bishops safeguard the authenticity of this faith.

Roman Catholics believe that the sacred Scriptures contain the word of God and because they are inspired, they are truly the word of God. The four Gospels occupy a central place because Christ is their centre. The task of interpreting the word of God, whether in Scripture or tradition, is entrusted to the bishops in communion with the Bishop of Rome. The bishops also exercise their teaching authority through the councils of the church. Roman Catholics profess their faith through the creeds, particularly the Apostles' and Nicene Creeds.

ROMAN CATHOLIC MISSION

Roman Catholics believe that the Church is by nature missionary, and that the task is to bring all to share in the communion between Father and the Son in the Spirit of love. Roman Catholics believe this is not only brought about by proclamation, but by trying to live as Christ did in loving service to all, and in obedience to the word of God.

ROMAN CATHOLIC PRAYER AND WORSHIP

The Roman Catholic tradition gives primary though not exclusive importance to the prayer of the church when it is gathered together to pray as the body of Christ. Above all this is the case when the parish community gathers for the Sunday Eucharist or Mass. The Eucharist is the chief sacrament. Bread and wine is taken in memory of the last supper Jesus took with his friends before he was arrested and crucified. Roman Catholics believe that in this solemn remembering the death and resurrection of Jesus are made present for them here and now, though in a different and sacramental way, and that they are united with him in his supreme act of self-giving to the Father, offering themselves and their lives to him.

They believe that by his power the bread and wine that we eat and drink have become, in a real but utterly mysterious way, his body and blood. The Mass, like the whole of Christian faith and discipleship, is deeply personal but never private. It is the action of a community rather than a gathering of individuals. The 'Amen' at the reception of the body and blood of Christ accepts all that the Catholic Church is. It is the body of Christ receiving the body of Christ.

Roman Catholics draw strength from non-eucharistic worship such as the stations of the cross and the rosary. They also have a tradition of praying before the Blessed Sacrament exposed (the reserved Eucharist).

As well as collective prayer, the Roman Catholic Church lays great emphasis on personal prayer, believing that all are called to be holy, as Christ is holy. Prayer may be in a set form of words, words personally chosen or in a wordless silence of love and worship. Prayer may be intercession in time of need, or of repentance, thanksgiving or simple wonder and adoration. Believing in the communion of saints – those who have gone before and come after them – Catholics have devotion to the saints both known and unknown. They pay special honour to Mary, the Mother of Jesus and Mother of God.

ROMAN CATHOLIC SACRAMENTS

A 'sacrament' is a sacred sign which, by the power of Christ, actually brings about what it signifies. Baptism is the sacrament that begins the process of initiation into Christ's Church; this process is continued in the sacrament of confirmation and is completed in the Eucharist or Holy Communion.

Other sacraments are to do with healing in sickness (anointing of the sick), forgiveness of sins committed after baptism (sacrament of reconciliation) or to mark life commitment, such as marriage and Holy Orders.

ROMAN CATHOLIC PARTNERSHIP IN THE ECUMENICAL JOURNEY

At the Second Vatican Council, in the 1960s, the Roman Catholic Church committed itself to the ecumenical movement.

The Holy Spirit is at work today causing people everywhere to pray and work for Christian Unity – that unity so greatly desired by Christ. This Council urges all Catholics to co-operate fully with this grace and to devote themselves actively and intelligently to the work of Ecumenism.

(*Decree on Ecumenism of the Second Vatican Council*)

In 1989 the Catholic Bishops' Conference of England and Wales voted unanimously to belong to Churches Together in England and Churches Together in Britain and Ireland and is fully engaged at all levels of ecumenical activity and dialogue in the four nations. The *Catechism of the Catholic Church* (1992) includes the ecumenical dimension as part of the basic teaching for all the faithful of the church. This was followed in 1993 by the *Directory for the Application of Principles and Norms on Ecumenism*, issued by the Pontifical Society for the Promotion of Christian Unity. An accessible version of the *Directory*, prepared by the Bishops' Conference Committee for Christian Unity has been approved by the Pontifical Council (see 'Useful Sources of Information').

Pope John Paul's encyclical *Ut Unum Sint* (1995) followed by his pre- and post-millennium encyclicals continue to make clear the Roman Catholic Church's commitment to Christian unity. The Committee for Christian Unity has prepared a 'Declaration of Ecumenical Welcome and Commitment' possible for use by those Roman Catholic congregations that are the only worshipping congregation in a particular place. They have also issued 'Guidelines for Catholics responding to Ecumenical Welcomes' from other denominations. These two documents have been published and distributed to all dioceses.

The Roman Catholic Church is engaged in dialogue with many other Christian traditions both nationally and internationally. In England the work of the English Anglican–Roman Catholic Committee (ARC) and of the British Methodist–Roman Catholic Committee mirror at national level the work of their international counterparts, the Anglican–Roman Catholic International Commission (ARCIC) and the International Methodist–Roman Catholic Dialogue.

The Revd Father Bernard Longley
Catholic Bishops' Conference of England and Wales

THE SALVATION ARMY

The Salvation Army originated in England as an evangelistic agency in the afterglow of the great Christian awakenings during the middle of the nineteenth century. These revivals spanned the Atlantic and transformed much of church life. With the Army's flexible command structure under the benign autocracy of its founder, the Revd William Booth, the movement spread rapidly beyond the confines of the British Isles from 1865. Today, the Salvation Army has evolved into an autonomous church operating in over a hundred countries worldwide, preaching the gospel in 173 languages and with an adult membership of more than 1 million soldiers and adherents.

The International Mission Statement of the Salvation Army states:

> The Salvation Army, an international movement, is an evangelical part of the universal Christian Church. Its message is based on the Bible. Its ministry is motivated by love for God. Its mission is to preach the gospel of Jesus Christ and meet human needs in his name without discrimination.

The official Year Book also contains a brief definition under the title: 'What is The Salvation Army?'

The Salvation Army is an integral part of the Christian Church, although distinctive in government and practice. The Army's doctrine follows the mainstream of Christian belief and its articles of faith emphasize God's saving purposes. Its objects are 'the advancement of the Christian religion . . . of education, the relief of poverty, and other charitable objects beneficial to society or the community of mankind as a whole' (Salvation Army Act 1980).

The rapid deployment of the first Salvationists was aided by the adoption of a quasi-military command structure in 1878 when the title, 'The Salvation Army', was brought into use. A similarly practical organization today enables resources to be equally flexible. Responding to a recurrent theme in Christianity that sees the Church engaged in spiritual warfare, the Army has used to advantage certain soldierly features such as uniforms, flags and ranks to identify, inspire and regulate its endeavours.

Internationally, the Army is governed by an elected General and the officers he or she appoints. The election is by a college of senior officers who meet as necessary for that purpose. The electoral procedures to be followed are set out in the Salvation Army Act 1980.

Evangelistic and social enterprises are maintained, under the authority of the General, by full-time officers and employees, as well as soldiers who give service in their free time. The Army also benefits from the support of many adherents and friends, including those who serve on advisory boards. Leadership in the Army is provided by commissioned officers who are recognized ministers of religion.

All Salvationists accept a disciplined and compassionate life of high moral standards, which includes abstinence from alcohol and tobacco. From its earliest days the Army has accorded women equal opportunities, every rank and service being open to them; and from childhood the young are encouraged to love and serve God.

Raised to evangelize, the Army spontaneously embarked on schemes for the social betterment of the poor. Such concerns have since developed wherever the Army operates, in practical, skilled and cost-effective ways. Evolving social services meet endemic needs and specific crises worldwide. Modern facilities and highly trained staff are employed.

Longer-term development is under continual review. Increasingly the Army's policy and its indigenous membership allow it to co-operate with international relief agencies and governments alike. The movement's partnership with both private and public philanthropy will continue to bring comfort to the needy, while the proclamation of God's redemptive love offers individuals and communities the opportunity to enjoy a better life on earth and a place in Christ's everlasting kingdom.

The teaching of the Salvation Army is regulated by its eleven articles of faith which originated in the doctrinal definitions employed by the Methodist churches from which it sprang. In addition to these articles, the Army recognizes its doctrinal roots in the historic creeds of the Church and considers these great achievements of the church fathers as the governing understandings of the Christian faith. The doctrine of the Trinity and of the two natures of the Lord Jesus Christ are taught as fundamental to Christian belief.

The Army's articles of faith are the theological basis on which Salvation Army soldiers are accepted and sworn in as full members. These articles are appended to the Salvation Army Act 1980 and are consequently part of the Army's legal constitution. Where similar legal instruments are in force in other countries where the Army operates, the same articles of faith are incorporated.

The Salvation Army was a founder member of the World Council of Churches. Since the late 1970s it has adopted a less formal linkage, initially in protest against what was interpreted as a politicization of the WCC. The Army retains a fraternal relationship within the WCC and has membership, world wide, with a variety of ecumenical bodies.

In the United Kingdom the Army is a member of Churches Together in England as well as the Welsh and Scottish equivalent bodies. The Army has non-governmental organization (NGO) status with the United Nations Organization and is a partner in many humanitarian and relief operations throughout the world.

The Army's form of worship centres around preaching from the Scriptures. The worship services reflect the ethnic styles of the various peoples among whom it operates. However, the Bible is always read and expounded. Preaching aims for decision and commitment on the part of the worshippers. A mercy seat, or penitent form, is a focal point of all worship halls. This seat is a bench, usually between the platform area (where is the meeting leader's rostrum) and the congregation's seats. At this mercy seat, people are invited to kneel in prayer and so publicly to affirm their obedience to God's moving in their lives. At the mercy seat, seekers may accept salvation by faith in Christ, receive the grace to live a Christian life, or express commitment to a particular Christian vocation. The mercy seat is not seen as having any intrinsic virtue, but is regarded as a place of prayer, hallowed solely by its use as a meeting place between a seeker and the living God.

Music has always been a rich and rewarding feature of Salvation Army worship. In the United Kingdom, brass bands, contemporary music groups, songsters (choirs) as well as other choral and instrumental combinations may feature. Extempore prayer and testimony is used, all members of the congregation being at liberty to contribute.

From its earliest years, all ages and both sexes have been encouraged to participate in worship and service. Army officers, as ministers of religion, lead worship and conduct ceremonies. Infants are dedicated to God though, if parents wish, a simple service of thanksgiving for the child may be used.

Marriages and funerals are also conducted by officers. Soldiers are formally received into full membership by a swearing-in ceremony, which includes their public affirmation of the articles of faith and the lifestyle ethics of Salvationism. An often-remarked feature of a soldier's commitment is a pledge not to use alcohol, tobacco or any non-medical drug. A form of membership as an adherent is currently available for those not wishing to make the full promises, but adherents state that they regard the Army as their church, and are expected to maintain Christian standards in their lives. Children are encouraged to commit their lives to Christ and in a simple formal declaration say that Jesus has saved them and that they will live as

Christians: daily prayer, Bible-reading and good living being emphasized.

In the United Kingdom, an appointed territorial commander is the chief executive officer, assisted by officers and others. As in all territories, the command is divided into geographical divisions, the equivalent of a diocese, the divisional commander being responsible for the work in his, or her, area in a similar way to that of a bishop. Advisory boards, comprised of friends of the Army with expertise in a variety of skills, including finance, form a valuable resource. Consultation within the Army at all levels, and on a variety of topics, is provided by ad hoc councils made up of officers and lay Salvationists.

The Army increasingly seeks and fosters good relations with other Christian denominations, recognizing the value of co-operation in many areas: evangelistic as well as in social work and legislative advice to assist governments. From its earliest days, the Army's policy has been not to criticize the practice or beliefs of other churches. It has been a source of regret, therefore, when Salvationists have been regarded as less than Christians for not observing some form of the two sacraments of water baptism and the Eucharist. The Army's position on these sacraments is not dissimilar from that of the Society of Friends (Quakers), and reflects a strand of Christian belief evident through the Christian millennia despite often bitter persecution by some fellow Christians. The Salvation Army's *Handbook of Doctrine* emphasizes that Salvationists receive the one, true sacrament, which is our Lord and Saviour Jesus Christ.

Salvationists believe that the baptism of the Holy Spirit (John 1.32–3) and the sacralizing of every meal at which the presence of Christ and true Christian fellowship are enjoyed, ensures that they are a truly sacramental people. The liberty of God to sacralize myriad experiences in life with the divine serendipity of his grace is thankfully acknowledged. In stating our position the Army implies no criticism of any communion blessed and enriched by sacramental observances, whether these number two or seven.

During the twentieth century, the Salvation Army in Europe suffered a decline in membership in common with most other Western churches. In other parts of the world significant growth is currently experienced so that internationally there are now more Salvationists than ever before. The Army has also benefited from the movements of renewal through the presence and gifts of the Holy Spirit. The spiritual integrity of Salvationists has been quickened thereby. The

Army rejoices in every gift and grace, which it recognizes in all contemporary expressions of Christian faith, and has every confidence in the sovereignty of God and the lordship of Jesus Christ. In concert with Christians everywhere, Salvationists look for the coming of his everlasting kingdom and, in obedience to his love, work towards that great and glorious consummation of our Lord's work on the cross.

Major Alan Dixon
Salvation Army

SMALLER FREE CHURCHES

ASSEMBLIES OF GOD

With doctrine based on evangelical fundamentals, in addition Assemblies of God stress the importance of baptism in the holy Spirit witnessed by the initial evidence of speaking in tongues. They are part of the modern Pentecostal movement, arising from the rediscovery of gifts of the Spirit (tongues, miraculous works of healing) in the early twentieth century. The service book, *A Manual for Ministers* (joint publication with Elim Pentecostal Churches, 1993) is also used for occasional offices.

The congregations in England are linked with Assemblies of God fellowships in most countries of the world, and the total enrolled membership in Britain and Ireland is 58,500. There are about 650 local congregations, referred to as 'assemblies', mostly in urban settings. Assemblies call their own ministers, who have often been trained at Mattersey Hall or other Bible colleges. Worship has a natural, not an imposed order, with songs and hymns from evangelical and Pentecostal sources, biblical preaching and periods of prayer with speaking in tongues. Baptism is administered to believers by immersion.

The assemblies are organised in thirteen geographic regions, each with a superintendent and council, and a national superintendency with a general superintendent for Great Britain and Ireland. There are about 880 accredited ministers. Some of the local assemblies, which vary greatly in size, belong to and work with their local Churches Together.

Their mission statement is: 'The purpose of Assemblies of God is to give every man, woman and child the opportunity of understanding the Gospel and to provide a church where they can grow and develop in ministry for the glory of God.'

THE COUNTESS OF HUNTINGDON'S CONNEXION

Based in the Calvinist evangelical theology of George Whitefield and the pre-Wesleyan Methodist movement, this connexion of twenty-three churches, mainly in south-east England, and a similar number in Sierra Leone is held together by a single body of trustees and annual conference. Congregations choose their own style of worship and call their own pastors (subject to approval by the trustees). Warm local fellowships, many long established in village and small town settings, resemble Congregational churches in their life and activity.

The unusual name of this small denomination derives from the dominance of Selina, Lady Hastings, in their early history by benefactions, foundation of chapels and appointment of chaplains. Although founded by a woman, there has not yet been a woman appointed to be a minister in the Connexion's churches.

While not in principle opposed to the baptism of infants, the practice is in decline.

The average membership of a local congregation, whose name and notice board will not necessarily refer to the Countess of Huntingdon, is thirty adults with a number of children.

THE FELLOWSHIP OF CHURCHES OF CHRIST

The Churches of Christ united in this fellowship, which should not be confused with sects bearing similar names, stem from a nineteenth-century development in the church life of Scotland, Northern Ireland, England and the USA, which sought to restore aspects of New Testament church practice. The founders mostly came out of the variety of Presbyterian churches at that period, and from the beginning there was a strong emphasis on the search for church unity.

Churches of Christ celebrate the Lord's Supper each Sunday as their main service. Membership is by immersion of believers and on profession of faith in Jesus Christ and Churches of Christ do not practise infant baptism.

Each local congregation is self-governing under elders and deacons who continue in their ordinary occupations. Some churches employ full-time ministers. It is usual for an elder or deacon to preside at the Lord's Table even when there is a minister, though he will also take a turn at presiding on some Sundays. There is always a time of open prayer. Churches practise what is known as 'mutual ministry' with several people taking part in the Communion service and any competent member may preach.

Government of the local church is by elders and deacons and the church meeting of all the members. The churches combine together in the Fellowship of Churches of Christ but the annual conference has no powers to overrule the independence of the local church.

A number of the Churches of Christ unified with the United Reformed Church in 1981; the fellowship includes thirty-two congregations, mostly in the Midlands, which did not do so.

The fellowship maintains links with Churches of Christ (often called 'Disciples of Christ') in the USA, Australia, parts of Africa and other countries.

THE FREE CHURCH OF ENGLAND

The worship style of the Free Church of England is close to that of a traditional evangelical Church of England parish, using a variant of the 1662 Book of Common Prayer. Emphasis is given to the Holy Scriptures of both Testaments as the word of God and sole rule of faith and practice. Regarding the Holy Communion as a memorial of Christ's death and passion, they maintain an 'open table'.

The Free Church of England adheres to the three ancient creeds of the Church and to their own revised version of the Thirty-nine Articles of Religion. Arising from strong opposition to the Tractarian movement and imposition of theologically unpopular clergy by patrons, without regard to local feeling, the Free Church of England began in 1844 and later united with congregations of the US-based Reformed Episcopal Church. The episcopal succession stems from Scotland through North America.

The Northern and Southern provinces embrace twenty-seven congregations and forty-four clergy. Four bishops (one appointed by his brethren to be the primus) provide oversight and leadership to the two convocations.

INDEPENDENT METHODIST CHURCHES

Methodist in doctrine but Congregational in government, the Independent Methodists rely on local initiative and lay involvement. They are evangelical in tone, ecumenical in spirit, and often ally themselves with other like-minded local churches in outreach and social action.

The Independent Methodist Churches seceded from the Wesleyan Methodist Churches and remained independent when the Methodist Church was united in 1932. They are mainly concentrated in the industrial areas of the north of England.

The ministry is open to both men and women and is unpaid. There are just under a hundred congregations and 2,500 members. The congregation's meetings and business are often presided over by an elected member who is not a minister.

The Independent Methodist Connexion maintains friendly relationships with the Wesleyan Reform Union, the Countess of Huntingdon's Connexion and the Baptist Union of Great Britain.

THE WESLEYAN REFORM UNION

Evangelical piety typifies the Wesleyan Reform Union, whose songs and hymns are typical of those sung in other evangelical churches. Concentrated in industrial Yorkshire and the Midlands, over 100 churches are served by only twenty ministers. The doctrine is Methodist but the polity and ministerial practice are more Congregational. The theological stance may be described as 'conservative evangelical'. The average congregation has twenty members.

Each church is autonomous, governed through its church members' meeting. Local preachers as well as ministers administer the sacraments of baptism and the Lord's Supper. Churches are arranged in circuits, but without superintendent ministers.

The Revd Geoffrey Roper
Associate General Secretary, Free Churches, CTE

THE UNITED REFORMED CHURCH

The United Reformed Church is both young and old. It was formed in 1972 out of the union of the Congregational Church in England and Wales and the Presbyterian Church of England. These were Reformed and dissenting churches with their roots in the sixteenth- and seventeenth-century reformations in England, Wales and Scotland.

As a united church, the United Reformed Church continued to express its commitment to the visible unity of the 'one holy catholic and apostolic church' through its union, in 1981, with the Re-formed Churches of Christ and, in 2000, with the Congregational Union of Scotland. Locally, almost one quarter of its 1,750 congregations are single congregation Local Ecumenical Partnerships – 200 with the Methodist Church; sixty with the Baptist Union; twenty-three with the Church of England; a few with the Moravian Church, the Presbyterian Church of Wales and the Church of

Scotland; and many more in partnership with two or more of these churches.

Although one of the smaller of the historic British churches, with a membership of 95,000, the United Reformed Church stands in the Reformed tradition whose members make up the largest single strand of Protestantism in the world – more than 70 million members. It confesses the Trinitarian faith of the Church catholic, and acknowledges that the life of faith to which the Church is called is a gift of the Holy Spirit continually received in word and sacrament and in the common life of God's people. It acknowledges the word of God in the Old and New Testaments, discerned under the guidance of the Holy Spirit, as the supreme authority for the faith and conduct of all God's people. It believes that through the preaching and the study of the Scriptures God makes known his saving love, his will for his people and his purpose for the world. Many local churches have Bible-study groups. When there is serious debate within the United Reformed Church, such as that concerning homosexuality, it is to the Scriptures that the church first turns.

In the United Reformed Church the gospel sacrament of baptism is the sacrament of entry and is therefore administered only once. However, following the union with the Re-formed Churches of Christ, the United Reformed Church honours the convictions of both those who believe that baptism can only be appropriately administered to a believer and those who believe that infant baptism is also in harmony with the mind of Christ.

The United Reformed Church celebrates the gospel sacrament of the Lord's Supper where the Lord is present and gives himself to his people for their spiritual nourishment and growth in grace. United there with him and with the whole Church on earth and in heaven, his people present their sacrifice of thanksgiving and renew the offering of themselves, and rejoice in the promise of his coming in glory.

The Lord's Supper is normally celebrated monthly, in some churches weekly or fortnightly and, in a few churches, quarterly. The United Reformed Church keeps an 'open table', often inviting 'all who love the Lord Jesus' to receive the bread and wine. This invitation can, by local decision, include children. The celebration of the Lord's Supper is normally accompanied by the hearing and the expounding, however briefly, of the Scriptures. An ordained minister normally presides, but elders may be authorized by the district council to preside where there is pastoral need. The bread and wine are usually, but not invariably, distributed by elders to the seated congregation.

Although worship in the United Reformed Church has all the major elements of worship in the Church catholic – praise and adoration, confession of sin and words of absolution, the Lord's Prayer, the hearing and the expounding of the word of God as it is contained in the Old and New Testaments, the offering of prayers of petition, dedication and intercession and also of money, bread and wine, the celebration of the sacraments of baptism and the Lord's Supper, the dismissal with a blessing – those leading worship may draw on written material of many traditions and cultures or lead in extempore prayer. Many leaders of worship follow the *Revised Common Lectionary*, but there is no requirement to do so. The *United Reformed Church Service Book* offers suggested orders of service. The only required wording, apart from the legally required marriage vows, is that for the promises made at baptism, on reception into membership and at the ordination and induction of elders and ministers.

The Apostles' and Nicene Creeds and the other formulations of faith produced in our particular traditions are not used regularly in worship. When United Reformed Church people confess their faith together in words they prefer to do so through hymnody, using hymns from within their own tradition, from Isaac Watts to Brian Wren, as well as hymns from many other Christian families. It is also a Reformed conviction that the Church is called to grow continually in its obedience to Christ, and the United Reformed Church therefore reserves the right, under the guidance of the Holy Spirit, to make new declarations of faith. The most recently formulated was accepted in 1997.

The United Reformed Church is, like all Reformed churches, a conciliar church, believing that by participation in the common life of the local church, members enter into the life of the Church throughout the world. Authority, oversight and pastoral care are exercised by a series of councils – the church meeting and elders' meeting in the local congregation, the district council, the synod, the General Assembly – each with its particular responsibilities. Those who are received into membership of the United Reformed Church are admitted to its 'privileges and responsibilities'. These are listed as 'to be faithful in private and public worship, to live in the fellowship of the church and to share in its work, and to give and serve, as God enables you, for the advancement of his kingdom'. The church meeting – for all members and held at least four times a year – is the key local expression of this participative understanding of church membership. Most decisions relating to the local church and its life and witness rest with the church meeting.

For the equipment of the whole people of God for their ministry and discipleship, the United Reformed Church recognizes that the Lord Jesus Christ gives particular gifts and calls some of his servants to exercise those gifts in offices duly recognized by the church. Some are called to be ministers of word and sacraments. After approved preparation and training they are ordained and inducted to their office. Some are called to be elders. They share with the minister of word and sacraments in the pastoral and spiritual oversight and leadership of the local church. They take counsel together in a monthly elders' meeting, and groups of members are entrusted to each elder's care. Elders are chosen by the members of the local church, ordained to their office and inducted to serve for such period as the local church determines. Elders and ministers together form all the wider councils of the United Reformed Church. All ministries in the United Reformed Church are open to both women and men.

In a 'vacancy' the district council appoints an interim moderator to help and guide the church, but continuity in ministry – arrangements for leadership of worship, pastoral care and the oversight of the life and mission of the church – is provided by an elders' meeting.

The district council – which usually meets quarterly and on which each church is represented by the minister and, normally, an elder – has considerable authority in some key areas; such as the oversight and deployment of ordained ministers, the financial assessments for local churches, and the regular review of the churches. It oversees the life of the churches through regular visits and it has to agree that a local church may call a minister, and then has to concur in the particular call. With the increasing number of churches grouped under one minister or a ministry team, the district council's oversight role is becoming more important.

The synod and the synod moderator exercise leadership rather than authority. There are thirteen synods, eleven in England and the national synods of Scotland and Wales. The moderator has a unique overview of the synod area. He or she offers pastoral care to the ministers, support to the district councils, and has a key facilitating role in the matching of ministers to churches. The moderator also plays a significant ecumenical role through the church leaders' meetings that fall within the synod area. Resource people for local church life – such as mission enablers, youth and children's work trainers and training officers – are mostly synod appointments. The synods meet twice yearly.

The General Assembly, meeting annually, acts as the central organ of the life of the United Reformed Church, is the final authority on all matters of doctrine and order and has ultimate authority for the common life of the church.

A sense of being part of the world Church and its mission is very much part of the ethos of the United Reformed Church. It plays its part in world mission through the Council for World Mission. This thirty-two-member council consists of churches in every continent founded by Congregational and Presbyterian and Churches of Christ missionaries and of the British churches which sent them. The United Reformed Church is a committed member of the World Council of Churches, the World Alliance of Reformed Churches, the Disciples Ecumenical Consultative Council and the Conference of European Churches. It has a strong sense of being a European church and has long-standing relationships with many of the Reformation churches in mainland Europe. It was one of the very early members of the Leuenberg Fellowship of Lutheran and Reformed Churches. It also has a special relationship with its various partners in the USA.

The United Reformed Church is both a broad and an inclusive church, open to new ways of declaring the Christian faith and of being Church in response to the demands of the gospel in a particular context. It is committed to the unity of all God's people as a witness both to God's nature and to the reconciling power of the gospel. Its Reformed heritage speaks of the crucial importance of the Bible and of the way personal faith must be expressed in the worship and the common life of the local church.

The Revd Sheila Maxey
Secretary for Ecumenical Relations, United Reformed Church

WHO ARE YOUR PARTNER CHURCHES?

The amazing variety of churches described above is really the outstanding feature of ecumenical life in England. In other northern European contexts, which are otherwise quite like our own, this variety is very unusual. Most of our close European neighbours have either a majority church that accounts for over 90 per cent of the population, as in Finland or Sweden; or a mix of churches across the nation, but which are each dominant in particular regions, as in Germany. Although there are few communities in England where you would find the complete range described above, in most centres of population there are a variety of traditions, and most congregations also contain people who have come from a variety of Christian traditions.

This denominational variety means that we have an almost unique opportunity to develop relations across a range of partners in the ecumenical process, which is very unusual. However, those churches that have been working together for unity for almost a century often find that their ecumenical activity is focused around a particular agenda, which they share but which does not help them to reach out to include in their fellowship those churches which have not, in the past, been a part of it. When in 1990 the new ecumenical structures came into being, they included some churches that had not been part of the previous structures and that represent a large proportion of the Christians in this country; for example, the Roman Catholic Church and black majority churches. As these churches came into membership of the instruments, a new energy for working for unity was released and agendas began to be reshaped to meet the concerns of these partners. Each time a new partner church joins the Churches Together process, at whatever level, that process will change as they bring different emphases, insights and challenges.

In recent years another group or family of churches has become increasingly involved in the ecumenical structures – those that are sometimes called 'community', 'house' or 'new churches'. With their evangelical orientation, these churches often become involved in the ecumenical structures when local Churches Together undertake mission or outreach projects, or where a particular event in the area brings them into the process. In many places Pentecost 2000 celebrations proved to be a catalyst that enabled the participation of these churches, and demonstrated to them the value of unity in mission. Some of those churches that have traditionally been part of the ecumenical scene have been renewed in their understanding of the importance of common mission recently. As this has happened, so many of the new churches have come to a growing realization that the unity of both the church and the human community – what are sometimes called kingdom issues – are profoundly important aspects of the gospel.

Some existing Churches Together groups struggle to develop

their agenda to reflect the concerns of new partners, but there is an example from the West Country that shows how churches can be renewed together through a healing of memories, calling for mutual generosity and forgiveness, and where a community church has been the catalyst for changed relationships within an existing Churches Together:

> In a large market town, the long-established Churches Together group plodded on through an agenda that focused on a round of ecumenical activities. Relationships were warm and friendly, with shared worship, social events, Lent groups and a ministers' fraternal. All the six churches that then participated in the Churches Together have buildings that were situated within the ring road, built about thirty years ago, although most of their congregations drove in on Sunday mornings as few people now live in the town centre. These congregations were all thriving, each with busy midweek programmes although they shared some social projects. Beyond the ring road were the church premises of what had been a Brethren congregation. In 1980, this church became affiliated to one of the networks of new churches, but although their worshipping life was being renewed their attitude to ecumenism remained cool. Then three members of this church, who were part of a prayer group, read John 17 together, and felt inspired to begin to pray for Christian unity in the town. Over the next fifteen years they continued this hidden ministry, and over that period a new generation of ministers was appointed to churches in the town, each with a greater degree of commitment to Christian unity than their predecessor.
>
> In the mid-1990s the churches that were members of the Churches Together were surprised to be contacted, one by one, by the Community Church. To each of these churches, the Community Church issued an invitation to join them at evening worship. In the course of these services the Community Church offered repentance that they had previously not fully appreciated the importance of Christian unity, and asked for forgiveness and a new beginning in the relationship. This honesty and generosity has spawned a new quality of relationship between all the churches, and the Churches Together is now quite a different kind of body – with much less focus on a round of ecumenical activities and more concentration on sharing in mission to meet the needs of the town.

There are, of course, plenty of places where churches that are often beyond the ecumenical circle have participated for many years in the local Council of Churches or Churches Together; but in some of those places where this has not been the case, and where there may have been pan-evangelical structures that rivalled the ecumenical ones, the celebrations around Pentecost 2000 do seem to have liberated some energy and understanding, which has renewed those churches in partnership for mission.

Exercise 2.1: Who Are Your Partner Churches?

Map out the existing patterns of church life in your area.

- Who are the partner churches in your area? (Don't forget those that may not have their own building, but share the building of another church, or use a school hall.)
- If you are already working with some other churches, which are the churches present in your area that are not currently part of this working for unity?

Look at how you are already working for unity.

- Are there existing ecumenical structures in your area? A Churches Together group? A Council of Churches? A Christian Aid Committee? A Week of Prayer for Christian Unity planning group? A ministers' meeting or fraternal?
- How effective do you think those structures are in helping the churches to work and worship together, and to develop their sense of common mission?
- How is your parish or church represented?
- How has working with partner churches changed or developed your church?

If there was one aspect of church life in your area which you could change, what would it be?

Exercise 2.2: How Did You Come to be Part of Your Church?

Is the church where you now worship the place where your faith has been nurtured for most of your life? If so, this is becoming an increasingly rare experience, as people move about the country for work or family reasons, and as they feel free to worship wherever they feel at home, without being tied so strongly by denominational allegiance as in the past. Also, as some traditions focus their work on market towns, many smaller communities in rural areas now have only one church building in active use, the congregation of which may be drawn from a wide variety of traditions. The same can be true of congregations in inner-city areas, and can represent a kind of ecumenism by default. With this greater ease of movement has come a breaking down of barriers between traditions, but not necessarily a cross-fertilization between them, as often happens when people who become part of another church then leave behind them the gifts and insights of their previous tradition.

People move from one church to another for all kinds of reasons:

- They might be spiritual. Peoples' needs in spirituality often change as they grow in the faith, and they may feel called to travel the next stage of their Christian journey in a different tradition.
- Sometimes they are doctrinal. For example, they may feel uncomfortable with developments in their church and see truths or values that are important to them upheld in another tradition, or they may come to a new understanding of the faith and the Church through the experience of another Christian tradition.
- They may be practical. The church building of a particular congregation may be on the best bus route, or there might be someone who can offer transport.
- The reasons might be to do with stages of life. A certain church might have a flourishing parent and toddler group, or a good Sunday school, or work with young people, or run a friendly afternoon fellowship.
- Another reason might be to do with friendships. A colleague from work might introduce you to their church when you are new to an area.

In the past, people tended to stay with the same tradition if they moved around, and that was usually the one in which they had been brought up; now that many people do not encounter Christianity until they are adults, they are more likely to become part of a particular church because it is nearby, or because a friend has introduced them or because they find there something which appeals to their temperament, spirituality or stage on the journey. The idea that we can choose, rather than inherit, our Christian tradition, is still a relatively new one.

If you have moved from one tradition to another, reflect on the following questions:

- What were the main reasons for your move?
- What are the things that attracted you to your present church?
- What are the main differences between your previous church and your present church?
- What did you find difficult or strange?
- What do you miss about your previous church?
- Are there any distinctive gifts, which were a part of the life of your previous church and which you would like to bring to your present church? (These might be things like particular hymns, forms of praying or preaching, spirituality or kinds of pastoral care of the congregation.)
- If you have moved from church to church a number of times – whether because you had to move from one place to another with your job, or because you were seeking different things from church life at different stages on your own pilgrimage – map out your journey, and think about the different patterns of church life that you have experienced.
- How could you share these experiences with your present congregation?

Think about the people you usually worship with. How many of them do you think have spent their whole worshipping life in one tradition? How does the variety of all these individual experiences help to shape the life of your church?

3
Are We Really Allowed to do This?

All the partner churches exist within frameworks of rules and definitions, which shape their lives and regulate the way they work. For some churches these rules are largely decided by the local congregation, while for others there are national or even international frameworks, and living within those frameworks is one of the things that define their belonging to a certain communion of churches. For some churches these rules will be called 'canon law', and may look rather like statute law at a cursory glance, while for others the definitions will be more overtly doctrinal. The differences between these ways of providing frameworks within which church life takes place are one of the clearest expressions of our different theologies of the Church:

- the place where the rules are made expresses something about the location of authority and decision making;
- the kind of definitions which we make about ourselves express the priorities of our tradition for order, doctrinal clarity or freedom of belief;
- the way in which such rules are put into practice is also important, since there is often more space for interpretation than one might think, but equally the things which turn out to be 'non-negotiable' can often surprise ecumenical partners.

CANON LAW AND HOW IT RELATES TO ECUMENICAL WORKING IN THE CHURCH OF ENGLAND

The single most important thing to understand about the Church of England's regulations on ecumenical working is that they are designed to give permission for ecumenical sharing in worship, rather than to prevent it. The canons were passed in 1989, at the end of a long process of drafting and consultation, and to a certain extent represent the provision of a framework, within the Church of England's law, that would support work that was already underway in many places. In other places the permissions of the canons have hardly been taken up at all, and many people, if they have heard of them, assume that they are only relevant to Local Ecumenical Partnerships (LEPs). In fact, Canon B43 relates to every place of worship in the Church of England, and is aimed to encourage parishes to share in worship with their partners, especially in situations where ecumenical relationships are developing, or where there is a shared pastoral concern, at baptisms, weddings and funerals. For many people who would like to develop relations with their partner churches there is still a lingering sense that, in worshipping together and inviting those from other churches to participate in leading worship, they are somehow breaking the rules, or going beyond what is really allowed or encouraged. The canons provide a framework within which Church of England people can participate with confidence in working for unity.

Below is an outline of the kind of invitations and permissions that are possible under the ecumenical canons. It is not a comprehensive statement of the canons, for which you should consult *Ecumenical Relations: Canons B43 and B44: Code of Practice* (The General Synod of the Church of England, 1989) and *Supplement* (1997). In some situations, what is possible in terms of ecumenical sharing is dictated not by the rules of the churches but by the law of the land. For example, the use of the buildings of other churches for weddings is almost impossible, unless they are covered by a formal sharing agreement, because of the provisions of the Marriages Act (1949).

CANON B43: A FRAMEWORK FOR SHARING WORSHIP

Canon B43 relates to every place of worship in the Church of England, and its provisions enable baptized members of other churches, who are in good standing, to participate in leading worship in the Church of England, if the minister or lay person is authorized to perform a similar duty in their own church:

- to say or sing Morning or Evening Prayer or the Litany;
- to read the Holy Scriptures at any service;
- to preach at any service;
- to lead the intercessions at the Holy Communion and to lead prayers at other services;
- to assist at baptism or the solemnization of matrimony or conduct a funeral service;

- to assist at the distribution of the holy sacrament of the Lord's Supper to the people at the Holy Communion.

Canon B43 sets out the permissions that must be obtained in extending such invitations: for most of these the agreement of the incumbent and the Parochial Church Council (PCC) is necessary, but for assisting at the Holy Communion or for an invitation to participate on a regular basis, the permission of the bishop is necessary.

The canon also provides for Church of England clergy, lay workers or Readers to accept invitations from partner churches to share in their worship, undertaking the roles that they perform in Church of England worship, providing that they have obtained the approval of the incumbent of the parish in which the service is to take place, together with the approval of the bishop and the PCC if the invitation is to take part in leading worship on a regular basis, or to participate in an ordination service or to preside at the Holy Communion.

In addition, the canon provides for the incumbent, with the approval of the PCC and the bishop, to invite members of the designated churches to use Church of England churches for worship in accordance with their own forms of service and practice, or for joint worship with the Church of England.

Canon B43 makes possible, within the framework of Church of England canon law, sharing in worship with partner churches. If very regular sharing is established, or hospitality in a Church of England building is needed week by week by a partner church, then it is advisable to explore the possibility of drawing up either an informal hospitality agreement, if the arrangement is temporary, or an agreement under the Sharing of Church Buildings Act and a Local Ecumenical Partnership if it is more long term. The county ecumenical officer and your diocesan (or other denominational) ecumenical officer will be able to advise you about this.

- Is your church already making use of Canon B43 to share in worship with ecumenical partners?
- How could the provisions of Canon B43 help to develop sharing in worship in your area?

CANON B44 AND LOCAL ECUMENICAL PARTNERSHIPS: ECUMENICAL EXCEPTIONS

The 1998 Lambeth Conference recognized the existence of what it called 'bearable anomaly'; not a very attractive description, especially if you live in an LEP, but an important and widely recognized principle that allows that on the way to full, visible unity, areas of church life will move forward at different speeds, and that in order to respond to particular contexts for ministry and to discover together the nature of the unity which is God's gift, exceptions will be made to the usual rules and patterns of the churches' lives. In England, LEPs represent the expression of this principle in the lives of the churches. In these exceptional situations, permission is given for experimenting with ways of being the Church across a number of traditions; for the Church of England the framework for this ecumenism of exception is provided by Canon B44.

Local Ecumenical Partnerships have their roots in informal areas of experiment and development in various dioceses during the early 1960s. In 1964, the British Faith and Order Conference, at Nottingham, called for the setting up of areas of ecumenical experiment, particularly as a response to areas of new housing, in new towns and elsewhere, being built in the post-war period. In the background to the 1964 conference were conversations between the churches, which led many people to hope that, before too long, the churches would come into new forms of unity with one another, through union schemes. Of the various talks, only that which gave birth to the United Reformed Church in 1972 bore immediate fruit, so the context of the areas, which from 1973 were called 'Local Ecumenical Projects', became one of a more long-term search for visible unity. Following the Swanwick Consultation on the future of LEPs in 1994, the name was changed again, to 'Local Ecumenical Partnerships', indicating the more permanent character of LEPs in many places.

The 1994 consultation agreed a definition of an LEP as existing 'where there is a formal, written agreement affecting the ministry, congregational life, buildings and/or mission projects of more than one denomination; and a recognition of that agreement by the sponsoring body, and by the appropriate denominational authorities'. This definition covers partnerships in an enormous range of contexts, including:

- single congregation LEPs, where several churches come together to share a building, ministry and church life;
- shared building LEPs, where one or more churches share a building, with a formal sharing agreement under the Sharing of Church Buildings Act, but continue some elements of their

lives separately, or where a community building is shared for
work together;

- covenant partnerships, where a number of existing churches
  work together as closely possible: these partnerships are sometimes called 'ecumenical parishes';
- partnerships which enable the churches to share in a project
  that serves the community or to undertake other work in the
  field of social responsibility, mission or Christian education;
  and
- chaplaincy partnerships, in schools, colleges, hospitals and
  prisons or in industry or agriculture.

What all these many different kinds of partnership have in common
is that they enable the churches to express their commitment to one
another, and to a place or common task, under God. Such commit-
ments are not usually made at the beginning of working together, but
rather express a maturity of relationship, which may have developed
over years of more informal contacts. People are sometimes unwilling
to think about setting up an LEP because they associate the process
with an excessive administrative burden, or with restrictions on their
work. In fact, if the partnership is appropriately established, with the
advice of the county ecumenical officer (CEO) and denominational
ecumenical officers, and with a declaration of intent, constitution
and sharing agreement that meet both local needs and the necessary
concerns of the sponsoring churches, then it is possible for LEPs to
provide a secure framework for developing relationships into the
future, releasing energy for mission and ministry together.

Canon B44 sets out the ways in which 'the bishop of the diocese
may enter into an agreement with the appropriate authority of each
participating church with regard to the participation of the Church
of England in an LEP'. So for the Church of England, an LEP exists
where:

- the bishop designates one
- with the approval of:
  - the incumbent
  - the PCC
  - an annual or special parochial church meeting
  - the diocesan pastoral committee
- in consultation with the deanery synod.

The bishop designates an LEP for a period of seven years at a time, and there will usually be a process for review before an LEP is re-designated for a further period.

Where an LEP is designated, the bishop may issue an instrument, which makes provision for ministry in the LEP and, in particular, authorizes:

- ministers of the participating churches to baptize in Church of England churches, using the rite of any participating church;
- a priest of the Church of England to preside in the LEP at a service of Holy Communion using the rite of any participating church;
- joint services, including services of baptism and confirmation; and
- the ministers of other participating churches to preside at services of Holy Communion in Church of England churches

within guidelines that ensure that it is always clear when worship is in the tradition of one of the other partner churches, and that neither the rite nor the elements depart from the doctrine of the Church of England in any essential manner. In addition, the canon sets out that Anglican worship should take place within the parish with reasonable frequency, and that there should be an Anglican service of Holy Communion (that is a service at which a priest of the Church of England, or an episcopally ordained priest of a church whose orders are recognized and accepted by the Church of England, presides) at least on Christmas Day, Ash Wednesday, Easter Day, Ascension Day and Pentecost.

A draft form for an instrument making provision for ministry in an LEP is available from the Council for Christian Unity.

Canon B44 also provides for the participation of cathedrals and institutions, such as schools and colleges, in LEPs. Canons B43 and B44 are published in a volume that includes detailed guidelines for the implementation of the canons and which is available from Church House Publishing.

SUPPORT AND REVIEW

The support and review of LEPs is shared by the churches through their involvement in the sponsoring body, which is usually the county or metropolitan Churches Together. The CEO is often the person who provides a routine contact with the LEP, sometimes in partnership with a local advisory group and with the denominational

ecumenical officers of the participating churches. There are a variety
of ways of providing support for LEPs, which of course need different levels and kinds of support in any case. Some sponsoring bodies
group LEPs together for mutual support, some ask members of the
sponsoring body to visit the LEP regularly on their behalf. In
undertaking reviews there is also a great variety of practice, including
review by teams appointed by the sponsoring body, self-review and
accompanied review. CTE publish *Guidelines for Reviewing Local
Ecumenical Partnerships* (CTE Group for Local Unity, 1999). Whatever patterns of support and review are adopted, what matters is that
they are appropriate to the nature and circumstances of the LEP and
meet the needs and expectations of the sponsoring churches,
enabling them to share in oversight of the LEP.

THE CHURCH AHEAD OF ITSELF?

One of the ways of understanding developing work for unity is in the
use of the 'C Scale', which charts relationships between churches in
a line which reaches from:

> Conflict to Competition to Co-existence to Co-operation to
> Commitment to Communion.

At the Swanwick Conference in 1987, the call was to move from co-
operation to commitment, but for almost forty years a section of
church life in England has been living in the borderlands between
commitment and communion, a situation that some in the churches
have found an anomaly that is hard to bear.

At their best, LEPs represent the church ahead of itself – saying,
in response to a particular place or piece of work, this place, this
agenda, is so important that we cannot allow the church's ministry
here to be impeded by the divisions of the churches. But the par-
ticularity of LEPs remains a problem, as well as a strength, as the
partner churches have found it hard to take on those insights, born
of this lived experience, into the unity of the church made visible in
a particular place and time, and apply them to broader contexts. In
their long development, from areas of ecumenical experiment
through projects to partnerships, LEPs have been a characteristic and
important part of ecumenical life in England, as well as quite a substantial part of English church life as a whole. The survey completed
in 2001 by CTE indicated that there are 861 LEPs of different
kinds in England. But LEPs have always been the ecumenism of

exception, and there are real questions about how this principle of bearable anomaly on the way to full, visible unity takes us forward in anything other than the very local situation, unless we are able to find more effective ways of listening to local experience.

If you would like to think about forming an LEP in your area, the CEO or your denominational ecumenical officer will be able to give you further information and advice. A helpful book on Local Ecumenical Partnerships is *Travelling Together: A Handbook on Local Ecumenical Partnerships* by Elizabeth Welch and Flora Winfield (CTE Publications, 1995). CTE also publish constitutional guidelines for LEPs, which have been agreed by the main sponsoring churches.

- Where, on the scale of conflict or competition to communion, would you locate relations between your church and partner churches?
- How could forming an LEP take forward partnership in worship, mission and service in your area?

DESIGNATED CHURCHES

The Ecumenical Relations Measure (1988) provides for the designation of those churches or councils with which the Church of England may work under Canons B43 and B44; designation is limited to those churches that subscribe to the doctrine of the Holy Trinity and administer the sacraments of baptism and Holy Communion. Work with those partner churches that do not administer these sacraments – the Salvation Army and the Society of Friends – is covered by an additional Guideline of the House of Bishops (1991). Churches that seek designation under the measure should belong to Churches Together in Britain and Ireland, the Evangelical Alliance or the British Evangelical Council and be gazetted under the Sharing of Church Buildings Act (1969) or be nominated by the General Synod for the purposes of the 1988 measure.

For further information on the process of designating a church or council, or an up-to-date list of designated churches, contact the Local Unity Secretary at the Council for Christian Unity. For information on gazetting under the Sharing of Church Buildings Act, contact the Church Life Secretary at CTBI.

Apart from the ecumenical canons, a number of other pieces of Church of England legislation relate to ecumenical working.

Growing Together

CANON B15A: ADMISSION TO HOLY COMMUNION (1972)

This enables baptized members of other churches to receive communion in the Church of England.

1 There shall be admitted to the Holy Communion:
   (a) members of the Church of England who have been confirmed in accordance with the rites of that Church or are ready and desirous to be so confirmed or who have been otherwise episcopally confirmed with unction or with the laying on of hands except as provided by the next following Canon;
   (b) baptized persons who are communicant members of other Churches which subscribe to the doctrine of the Holy Trinity, and who are in good standing in their own Church;
   (c) any other baptized persons authorized to be admitted under regulation of the General Synod; and
   (d) any baptized person in immediate danger of death.
2 If any person by virtue of sub-paragraph (b) above regularly receives the Holy Communion over a long period which appears likely to continue indefinitely, the minister shall set before him the normal requirements of the Church of England for communicant status in that Church.
3 Where any minister is in doubt as to the application of this Canon, he shall refer the matter to the Bishop of the diocese or other Ordinary and follow his guidance thereon.

THE CHURCHWARDENS MEASURE (2001)

This measure states the qualifications for being chosen as a churchwarden, stating that:

- each parish should have two churchwardens;
- churchwardens should be chosen from people who are on the church electoral roll of the parish, are actual communicants, are twenty-one years of age or older, and who are not disqualified; and
- if there are 'exceptional circumstances' whereby a departure from these requirements could be justified, then the bishop may permit a person to hold the office of churchwarden even if they do not meet the requirements, for periods of one year at a time.

Such circumstances might include a situation in a small village, where a Roman Catholic was worshipping regularly in the Anglican parish church, but also regularly attending Mass and therefore in good standing with their own church. Such a person would not be able to become an 'actual communicant', because of the discipline of the Roman Catholic Church, but could hold office as a churchwarden, if they seemed to the Church of England bishop to be the most suitable person to do so, and as long as the Roman Catholic bishop was also happy to give his permission.

THE CHURCH REPRESENTATION RULES (1995)

Rule 1 enables a person to remain a member of another church and also to be on the Church of England's Electoral Roll:

> 2. (c) to be a member in good standing of a Church which subscribes to the doctrine of the Holy Trinity (not being a Church in communion with the Church of England) and also prepared to declare himself to be a member of the Church of England having habitually attended public worship in the parish during a period of six months prior to enrolment.

'Public worship' means public worship according to the rites and ceremonies of the Church of England.

Rule 54 is the basis for a member of another church being described as an 'actual communicant' of the Church of England.

> 54. (1) In the Church Representation Rules:
> 'actual communicant' means a person who has received Communion according to the use of the Church of England or of a Church in communion with the Church of England at least three times during the twelve months preceding the date of his election or appointment being a person whose name is on the roll of a parish and is either –
> (a) confirmed or ready and desirous of being confirmed; or
> (b) receiving the Holy Communion in accordance with the provisions of Canon B15A paragraph 1.(b).

Given this understanding of participation in parish life, Rule 10 states who may be elected to the PCC or deanery synod:

> 10. (1) Subject to the provisions of Rule 1.(4) and sub-paragraph (3) of this rule, the qualifications of a person to be elected a parochial representative of the laity to either the parochial church council or the deanery synod are that –

(a) his name is entered on the roll of the parish;

(b) he is an actual communicant as defined in Rule 54.(1); and

(c) in the case of election to the parochial church council, he is of sixteen years or upwards, and in the case of his election to the deanery synod, he is of eighteen years or upwards.

Rule 31 then provides for deanery synod members to be the electorate in the elections to the diocesan synod and for the qualifications of those to be elected to the diocesan synod, and Rule 35 provides for deanery synod members to be the electorate in elections to General Synod. Rule 37 sets out the qualifications needed to stand for election to the General Synod.

Further information on these canons and rules is available from *A Handbook for Churchwardens and Parochial Church Councillors*, Kenneth M. MacMorran and Timothy Briden (Mowbray, 2001).

DECLARATIONS OF ECUMENICAL WELCOME AND COMMITMENT

The following declaration has been agreed by the House of Bishops.

WHEN THE ANGLICAN CHURCH IS THE ONLY CHURCH IN A VILLAGE

Suggestions and guidelines

1 In many villages there is only one church building and worshipping community, most often Church of England. Within the village there may be Christians of different traditions, some of whom try to combine loyalty to a particular denomination with their desire to worship and witness in their local community. Sometimes a church of another denomination has been closed, sometimes people from another denomination have moved into the village, sometimes those who previously commuted to a church outside the village are prevented from doing so through infirmity or poor public transport.

2 The aim of parochial church councils and incumbents will be to make members of other denominations feel at home in their local Anglican church, and to feel that they belong to the Christian community in that place. The sense of belonging and being valued may not for everyone be the same as 'being a member'. This is because not all those of other denominations are able, because of their denomination's rules, to declare

themselves also to be members of the Church of England (as the Church Representation Rules permit).

3 The church making this declaration, while remaining subject to the jurisdiction of the Church of England and guardian of its tradition, formulates a policy towards those of other denominations which enables their insights, strengths, gifts and graces to be incorporated into the whole life of the congregation. That life will include worship, mission and service, as well as the administrative and decision-making process.

4 There may be occasions when those of another denomination worshipping in the parish church wish to express their membership and belonging in a particular way. For example, when the tradition with which they have been familiar has a membership structure more closely defined than that of the Church of England. This could be expressed through a short welcome, prayer, and the right hand of fellowship which could take place at the Peace.

5 The congregation of the parish church will want to be especially aware of its responsibility to be broad, flexible and open, and to affirm a diversity of religious experience and expression. (This applies to the variety of emphases within a denomination, as well as between the various denominational traditions.) Breadth and openness could be affirmed through:

- choice of hymns, tunes, and hymn books;
- prayers for other churches and their leaders;
- invitations to ministers of other traditions to participate in leading worship or preaching (as allowed by Canon B43);
- occasional use of other denominations' liturgies (as allowed by Canon B43);
- occasional use of other practices of administering Holy Communion;
- careful use of language which includes and is not specific to one denomination;
- offering occasional (or regular) use of church buildings to other Christian traditions;
- use of non-eucharistic services to bridge divide of eucharistic hospitality between Roman Catholics and other churches;
- consultation between those with pastoral oversight in the area about the responsibility of care, initiation, nurture, etc.

6 Before a single church agrees a Declaration of Ecumenical

Growing Together

Welcome and Commitment it should seek advice from the 'Intermediate body' or its ecumenical officer as to which other denominations should be consulted, and at what level. The Group for Local Unity of Churches Together in England suggests that for the Methodist Church this should be the Circuit Superintendent and stewards, and for the United Reformed Church, the Church Secretary and the President of the District Council. Care needs to be taken over the real or imagined effect on the congregational strength of these churches, so that this is not seen as 'poaching'. Sensitivity is needed to the existence of small groups of Christians, who may be meeting for worship in local houses in some situations, so that this initiative is not perceived as Anglican imperialism. A copy of the Declaration should be displayed in the church.

A DECLARATION OF ECUMENICAL WELCOME AND COMMITMENT BY A CHURCH OF ENGLAND PARISH

1 We, the *Vicar* and people of *St CCC's*, are aware that *St CCC's* is the only church in *Aford*, and therefore we invite all Christians in *Aford* to be as fully a part of our life and fellowship as they are able.

2 We invite those of Christian traditions other than our own

  • to share in the ministry and mission of the Church in this community
  • to worship and, if baptized and communicant members of other churches, to receive Holy Communion at *St CCC's*,[1]
  • to be part of the decision-making of the church and to contribute to a common fund for the mission and ministry of the wider church in so far as their continued giving to another church will allow.[2]

3 We undertake

  • to give pastoral care to all those who desire it
  • to invite ministers of other churches to take part in leading worship[3]
  • to incorporate the riches of worship of other traditions as appropriate[4]
  • to consult with neighbouring churches concerning the mission of the church in *Aford*

- to include this ecumenical declaration as an integral part of the parish profile.

4 Following the decision made by Churches Together in *Ashire* (our 'Intermediate body') on .... 200*X* that such declarations may be made in the area which they serve, we have sought and followed their advice as to which churches should first be consulted, and those mentioned below have given us their blessing and encouragement.

for *St CCC's Aford*: *Vicar*: ....

Churchwardens: ....

for other churches: signature: ....

on behalf of: ....

1 Canon B15A (1972) enables the admission to Holy Communion of 'baptized persons who are communicant members of other Churches which subscribe to the doctrine of the Holy Trinity, and who are in good standing in their own Church . . .' If anyone by virtue of this provision 'regularly receives the Holy Communion over a long period which appears likely to continue indefinitely, the minister shall set before him the normal requirements of the Church of England for communicant status of that Church.'

2 The Church Representation Rules enable a person to be enrolled if she/he is baptized, sixteen years or upwards and declares themselves 'to be a member in good standing of a Church which subscribes to the doctrine of the Holy Trinity . . . and also prepared to declare himself to be a member of the Church of England having habitually attended public worship in the parish during a period of six months prior to enrolment.' Making this declaration, together with actual communicant status, also confers eligibility to stand for election to the decision-making bodies of the Church of England.

3 Canon B43 (1989) says 'A minister or lay person who is a member in good standing of a Church to which this Canon applies and is a baptized person may, subject to the provisions of this Canon, be invited to perform all or any of the following duties:
   a) to say or sing Morning or Evening Prayer
   b) to read the Holy Scripture at any service
   c) to preach at any service
   d) to lead the intercessions at the Holy Communion and to lead prayers at other services
   e) to assist at baptism or the solemnization of matrimony or conduct a funeral service
   f) to assist in the distribution of the holy sacrament of the Lord's Supper to the people at the Holy Communion if the minister or lay person is authorized to perform a similar duty in his or her own Church.

4 Canon B43 (1989) says: 'The incumbent of a parish may (with specified approval)

invite members of another Church ... to take part in joint worship with the Church of England or to use a church in the parish for worship in accordance with the forms of service and practice of that other Church on such occasions as may be specified in the approval given by the bishop.'

The Baptist Union, Roman Catholic, Methodist, Moravian and United Reformed Churches have also produced editions of the Declaration, for use in situations where theirs is the only church in a community. Copies are available from denominational ecumenical officers or national church offices. Some churches have also produced guidelines for their own members who are worshipping regularly with partner churches.

EXAMPLES

Perhaps the best way of illustrating the possibilities for ecumenical working is to look at some particular situations and see what is possible and how the framework for ecumenical relationships, provided by the canons, can enable working together.

In a remote rural valley, eleven villages that once each had a church and a chapel now have just the parish churches, and many of these have services only twice a month. A small team of clergy and Readers serve the valley parish, and are hard pressed. In the nearest market town, a Methodist chapel and a Baptist church draw their congregations from across a wide area. The Roman Catholic church is further away, and serves a huge parish.

A retired Baptist minister, living in one of the villages, worships each week in his parish church, and is much appreciated as a resident who knows and understands the life of the village. The churchwardens invited him to read the lessons occasionally, and then to lead the intercessions at the Holy Communion and to assist at the distribution of the elements, having sought the permission of the incumbent and the bishop, as necessary. After some time, they wrote to the bishop, asking whether it would be possible for this minister to preside at the Holy Communion from time to time, and he replied, giving permission under Canon B43.(9) for the minister to preside four times a year, using a Baptist rite.

In another village in the team, when one of the churchwardens retired it was very hard to find someone willing to take on the responsibility. Among those who attended the church was a

Methodist, who was a still a member of the chapel in the market town, but who had chosen to worship on three Sundays in each month in the village where she lived. She was a former circuit steward, and well used to taking responsibility in the church. After a discussion among the PCC, it was agreed that she was the obvious person to be the new churchwarden. The outgoing churchwarden asked her whether she was willing to serve in this role, and she said that she would be delighted, provided that she did not have to forgo her Methodist membership, which was still important to her. The PCC consulted the rural dean, who advised them about the Church Representation Rules, under which the Methodist could declare herself to be also a member of the Church of England, while retaining her Methodist membership.

Following an away day with the market town fraternal, the Anglican team rector telephoned the bishop, to ask whether he could invite the Roman Catholic parish to use one of the village churches as a place to celebrate Mass. The bishop replied that he would be happy to give permission, under Canon B43.(9), and advised the rector that it was a good idea to consult the DEO about putting together an informal hospitality agreement in such situations. The team rector and the parish priest met for lunch and, in discussing the villages, recalled that in one were a family where the husband was a Roman Catholic and the wife an Anglican. At their wedding, in the Roman Catholic church, the team rector had assisted and led the prayers. They now divided themselves between the two churches, going to Mass on Saturday evenings and the village church on Sunday mornings. In the village church they shared in running the Sunday school, which their own two children attended. The team rector and the parish priest visited the family, and asked whether they would be willing to act as hosts in their village church, welcoming people from other villages to Saturday evening Mass, co-ordinating Readers and a crèche and the children's liturgy. They agreed to take this on, on the condition that they give up their role in the Sunday school. The Mass is well attended, and worshipping so much nearer to their own community has helped a number of families to become more regular in their attendance.

In another of the villages, the Methodist chapel had closed in 1970, and the remaining twelve members had begun to attend the parish church, which welcomed them. The failure of the

Anglican–Methodist Union Scheme, in 1972, was a great disappointment but they continued to worship in the Anglican church, and the PCC erected a plaque to commemorate the 150 years that the Methodist chapel had served the village. In 1997 one of the Readers attended a day conference for deanery ecumenical representatives in the diocese, where he heard about the Declaration of Ecumenical Welcome and Commitment. At the next PCC meeting, he explained about the Declaration, and it was agreed that the village church should consult the partner churches locally about making a Declaration. One of the PCC members reminded the meeting that he had originally been a member of the Methodist Church, and the PCC decided that they should also consult the circuit about making this element in their village's history more explicit. The village church now appears on the plan of the Methodist circuit, and a minister or local preacher leads worship once a quarter, with the permission of the bishop under Canon B43.(1).

• How could the use of these permissions help to develop work for unity in your area?

4

What Does It Mean to be the People of God in This Place?

We believe that the unity which is both God's will and his gift to his Church is being made visible, as all in each place who are baptized into Jesus Christ and confess him as Lord and Saviour are brought, by the Holy Spirit, into one fully committed fellowship, holding the one apostolic faith, preaching the one Gospel, breaking the one bread, joining in common prayer and having a corporate life reaching out in witness and service to all; and who, at the same time, are united with the whole Christian fellowship in all places and all ages in such wise that ministry and members are accepted by all, and that all can act and speak together, as occasion requires, for the tasks to which God calls his people. (The message of the Third Assembly of the World Council of Churches, New Delhi, 1961)

The Church is not so large that the Christian community loses coherence, nor yet so small that its homogeneity favours separation in the human community. (*God's Reign and Our Unity*, The report of the Anglican–Reformed International Commission, 1984)

ALL IN EACH PLACE . . . IN ALL PLACES AND ALL AGES: WHAT DO WE MEAN BY 'LOCAL'?

The question of what exactly constitutes 'the local church' is a cause of some perplexity in ecumenical working. From ancient Christian tradition, local has been understood as being the church in the diocese, gathered around the bishop as the focus, sign and instrument of unity. For Roman Catholic, Anglican and Orthodox Churches, this is still their understanding of what constitutes the local church. For others, predominantly in the Reformation traditions, to speak of the local church is to think about the church at what might be called the very local level – the neighbourhood, the small settlement, the company of believers gathered in this place and moment. Of course, in early Christian times dioceses were geographically small, and grew larger as Christianity spread across Europe and, in the case of the Church of England, have been subdivided gradually ever since, in an irregular process towards being roughly the size of the English counties.

So, for the Church of England 'the local church' remains the diocese, even though in everyday conversation many people do refer to 'the local church' but mean the parish. For many Reformation traditions, everything that the Church needs to express the fullness of its life is already found in 'the local church', understood as being in a certain place and time; and fellowship and interdependence with other local churches, although important, is probably not essential in understanding the very nature of the Church itself. In Anglican understanding, to be 'the local church' is to hold together both a commitment to the church in a particular time and place – the parish – and an understanding of the Church's fullness as expressed when each particular time and place is held in unity with all places and all ages, through participation in the life of the diocese.

Clearly these different understandings of 'the local church' have considerable implications for what is usually called 'local ecumenism'. For the Methodist Church, the local is the circuit; for the URC and the Baptists it is the very local congregation, but they have very different structures for maintaining the interdependence of those congregations. In ecumenism in England – in spite of the very considerable presence of Anglicans and Methodists and, in more recent times, Roman Catholics – 'local' has almost always come to mean 'very local'. When we speak of Local Ecumenical Partnerships we often mean very local – a single congregation or a covenant partnership of churches in a defined area.

The point about this continuing conversation about 'local', and what it means theologically, is that attempts to understand the Church are always fundamentally bound up with the rest of the human community and its formation of settlements and places. When we say 'local' it must mean something to people – about belonging, location, community, identifiable space, shared culture – although these will not always be simply a matter of geography. In LEPs of both the single-congregation and covenant-partnership types and in Churches Together groups, the place where they are located is often the clearest and most influential factor shaping their life and nature, far more important than the particular combination of churches that they bring together, so that partnerships with the same mix of churches will be utterly different – as they are shaped in response to locality. LEPs and Churches Together groups in localities that have a strong sense of place, and that work with that dynamic, are usually effective. This is one of the reasons why there are so many lively partnerships in market towns, even in areas affected by many other adverse factors.

Locality must always mean something to people, but that meaning will not always be bound up with geography. Those churches that have an understanding of the church as fully expressed at the very local level have, for centuries, used a common culture and belief structure as a form of non-geographical locality. For them, the local church might be scattered across many settlements, but remains 'local' even when not physically gathered for worship. As whole communities now travel from where they sleep, and nominally live, to work, to school, to shop, to spend leisure time or to go to church, all the churches have increasingly to work with more fluid and less geographically defined ways of understanding 'local', as people discover a sense of 'local' belonging in networks, groups, on the Internet and as a concept which is no longer necessarily linked with a sense of place.

LOOKING AT YOUR LOCALITY
Exercise 4.1

- When you think of 'the local church', what do you have in mind?
- What effect do you think these different ideas of 'the local church' might have on the ways in which the partner churches can work together in your area?
- Looking at your local area, how do you think that it shapes any work that the churches do together?
- How do the partner churches together take account of needs and opportunities in your local community? Have you considered undertaking a mission audit of your local community together?

In Chapter 1, I talked about the way in which some churches working together have experienced a new sense of the imperative for unity in mission, as their focus has moved away from the relationship between the churches and towards a new, shared engagement with their local community. In asking together the question, 'What does it mean to be the people of God in this place?' the churches deliberately choose to work with a priority for the kingdom and for the needs of the world before the Church and, in working in this way, they begin to glimpse together something of what the unity of the Church might look like. Some time ago I was doing a review of a covenant partnership in a small town. There were some difficult conversations going on in the background to the review about whether there were too many church buildings in the town, and if so how this problem might be faced. I went with some of the people from the partnership on a post-review weekend away, where we spent time looking at the different churches and their gifts and needs. Afterwards, one of the clergy said to me,

> What I now understand is there are not eight churches in our partnership but one, whose life is expressed through the lives and traditions of eight congregations. And the life of that church must be about the mission of God in the town, and not about how the congregations fit together.

WAYS OF WORKING TOGETHER

Here are some examples of different ways of working together, in response to different contexts. I have disguised most of the situations, but they all reflect real places and experiences and I am grateful to those who, very generously, have told the stories of their experience and shared their reflections on it.

These examples reflect not only responses to different local situations, but also different ways of working together, in areas like lay training, mission or spirituality, and different methods of working. They are not intended to provide a comprehensive list of what is possible, but to illustrate some opportunities. Each example is followed by questions to stimulate your thinking, in relation to your own context.

IN WORSHIP

In a small industrial town, the Churches Together decided to move towards committing themselves to one another in a covenant partnership. As a part of this process, they reviewed their life together, which included a pattern of monthly evening ecumenical worship, which took place in the various churches but was always enabled by the same worship group, and always had roughly the same flavour. When they were initiated, ten years ago, these services were quite well attended, but numbers had fallen away and the Churches Together took the decision to change their pattern, and worship together less often and in the tradition of the host church on each occasion. The services are now held quarterly, and are well attended and much more diverse in form and content. Some members of the disbanded worship group have found this difficult, but others have expressed their appreciation of this chance to experience worship in the different traditions.

The partner churches also agreed that they should move towards having house groups that were based in the various areas of the towns, rather than in the separate congregations. Some rather long-standing house groups found the change difficult, and one of the churches, which had never had any house groups, found itself discovering a whole new culture. After a while, the house groups settled down to their programme of study and prayer, and as people lost their self-consciousness, they came to know one another as neighbours, and to pray for the local area where they lived in an entirely new way.

- How do the churches share worship, prayer and study in your area?

IN SPIRITUALITY

In a suburban area, the Churches Together group is made up of two Anglican, two Methodist and two Roman Catholic churches and a Quaker meeting. Among their other work and prayer together, sharing spirituality has always been an important strand in their relationship and every summer the churches undertake a pilgrimage together to a place of importance to one of the traditions. Together they have visited Epworth, Holy Island and Ampleforth Abbey, among other places. People from the churches have also shared a series of retreats in different spiritual traditions, including an Ignatian retreat in daily life, a weekend spent with a Benedictine community, and Saturdays that have provided an introduction to Quaker spirituality and to the hymns of Charles Wesley.

- How could churches in your area share their spiritual traditions?

IN MISSION – WITNESS AND SERVICE

The Churches Together in a large town undertook a mission audit together, and discovered a number of things that changed the focus of their work together. One of these was the extent to which under-age drinking was a problem in the town centre. After considerable discussion with local schools and with the youth worker who they jointly employed, the churches agreed to set up a non-alcoholic pub, called 'the King's Arms'. The town's Salvation Army officers were able to access specialist advice on the project, and the churches leased some empty restaurant premises in the town centre and employed a part-time project manager. The project has thrived, and has proved an important part of the churches' shared witness and service in the town.

In a new town, a church community worker worked on behalf of the Anglican, Methodist, URC and Baptist Churches and in partnership with two Salvation Army officers on a large and rather rundown estate. The community worker was very involved in the two schools, which struggled to find governors from among the local community, and much of his time was spent helping families who had problems with debt, housing or crime. The estate was much troubled by loan sharks, who lent money to families at exorbitant rates of interest and sometimes took away their benefit books. Together the community worker and the Salvation Army officers explored the possibility of setting up a credit union – a kind of community bank that would give the people from the estate access to savings and loan facilities and remove some of the threat of the loan sharks. A public meeting on the estate produced a good response, and the credit union was established, with a small committee of local people. As well as alleviating the financial problems of people from the estate, the credit union had two interesting by-products: as local people were trained to run the credit union, they were empowered to take control of other parts of their lives; and as they gained experience of serving on the credit union committees it became much easier to recruit them as school governors.

In the east of England the chairman of a Churches Together group challenged them, in his sermon at their annual service celebrating Christian unity, to join him in forming a group that would offer visits and caring work to people in the community. About twenty people from six of the partner churches attended an inaugural meeting, and agreed to set up the group 'Christian Care' to visit elderly people in their own homes and in residential care. The group also leads worship in a local day centre, and the members commit themselves to pray for those whom they visit.

In a suburban area, a long-established covenant partnership was approached by the probation service, with a request for help in setting up and running a contact project. This would provide a neutral, secure and welcoming meeting place for children and parents, helping to maintain contact in broken and troubled families. The churches provide a comfortable space, in a church hall, and volunteers who prepare refreshments and offer informal support, alongside professional staff. The volunteers also meet to pray for the contact project and those who use it.

- How could churches in your area identify needs within the local community to which they could respond together?

IN DOING THEOLOGY TOGETHER

In the west of England, a layman involved in his local Churches Together identified the need for a forum, to provide opportunities for lay people and ministers from the partner churches across the county to hear lectures from 'distinguished and forward-looking theologians' and to discuss them in groups, the aim being to provide a 'lively and stretching experience' in an ecumenical context. The forum is now organizing three well-attended lectures a year.

In a large market town, which is a covenant partnership, a review of the LEP identified that there was an opportunity in this well-established situation, with mature relationships between the churches, to undertake some theological reflection on the things that divide them. A Theology Together group was established, bringing together the clergy and ministers, but after several meetings there was some indignation that lay people were not also included. The group was expanded, and has shared a number of away days, led by people from different traditions, on aspects of their churches' theology. This has proved helpful in a number of other areas of the partnership's life, as people now have a better understanding of one another's theological outlook, and have found a new focus on the theological challenges of their shared context.

- What kind of opportunities to do theology together could help relationships and understanding in your area?

IN THEOLOGICAL EDUCATION AND TRAINING

Forming people for ministry in an ecumenical context is likely to have a significant impact on their future ministry. All the theological courses that offer part-time training for ministry now work ecumenically, as do most theological colleges. Queen's College in Birmingham is an ecumenical college, offering learning, praying and living together in an ecumenical context to candidates for ministry from the Church of England, Methodist Church and United Reformed Church, and working in partnership with the Roman Catholic Seminary at Oscott. There are also other patterns – for example, in Cambridge colleges from the Anglican, Methodist, URC, Roman Catholic and Orthodox traditions work together in a federation, while in Durham Anglicans, Methodists and Roman Catholics are taught together and work for the same degree.

In some places, Church of England Readers, Methodist local preachers and Baptist and URC lay preachers are trained together, and in others their in-service training is undertaken ecumenically. There are a number of ecumenical training schemes for lay people, which offer theological or pastoral education, or training for work with children or young people. In the Midlands, Church of England and Roman Catholic dioceses, a URC provincial synod and a Methodist district have together set up a programme called 'Christians Learning Together'. This offers a range of courses and day events, including basic belief, understanding renewal, an introduction to Christian mystics, courses on the Epistles and Gospels, and children's spirituality. The programme includes both courses that are organized jointly and courses that are run by each of the partner churches, and aims to complement what is provided by local churches.

A number of Churches Together groups also organize training opportunities. A good example is a cathedral city group, which organizes lectures during the winter on theological subjects, and offers training in more practical areas – such as listening skills, group work or improving reading Scripture in the liturgy – during the spring and summer terms. They have also run a number of quiet days, for people who have not made a retreat before, which have proved popular.

A small inner-city Churches Together group identified their training need as being enabled to understand their faith more fully and to share it more confidently. They have now run three six-week courses, enabled by a small team of clergy and lay people from other parts of the city.

- What opportunities for learning together are there in your locality?

IN TAKING COUNSEL TOGETHER

In the context of the formal conversations between the Church of England and the Methodist Church, the first joint meeting of the diocesan synod of the Anglican Diocese of York and the synod of the York and Hull District of the Methodist Church was held at Ampleforth Abbey in April 2000. A similar joint meeting has been held only once before, in 1971 when the diocese and district synods in Liverpool met together.

The two synods had a joint meeting during the morning and a final plenary in the afternoon after conducting separate business in the session after lunch. The joint meeting passed the following resolutions:

- This historic synod rejoices in the co-operation that is growing in a multitude of local communities, and commits itself to deepening our fellowship and life together in Christ.
- To this end, we wish to meet as a joint synod at least once in every two years.
- We urge the district and diocese to find the means of
  - identifying the problems that confront us
  - learning from existing good practice
  - involving as many other churches as possible in this venture.

Hospitality was also provided by Ampleforth Abbey in January 2000 for a meeting of the Church of England House of Bishops with the district chairmen of the Methodist Church. In many areas, Church of England deaneries and Methodist circuits have been exploring the possibilities for working together, with meetings of rural deans and superintendents and joint deanery synod/circuit meetings.

Some Intermediate bodies organize a regular county forum, once or twice a year, bringing together representatives from the churches, local Churches Together groups, LEPs and agencies like Christian Aid and CAFOD. These forums focus on a wide range of topics, in their different contexts, including:

- reports from localities about the churches working together, sharing ideas and good practice;
- issues of concern in local communities – such as rural stress or mission in the inner city;

- responding to national initiatives, or planning together.

They usually include time spent in worship and work in small groups as well as in plenary.

- How could the churches in your area begin to take counsel together, either through joint meetings of their synodical structures or through the Churches Together group, locally or at the Intermediate level?

IN CELEBRATING TOGETHER

A large market town was celebrating the six-hundredth anniversary of its market charter, with a year-long round of exhibitions and concerts, a carnival and children's activities. As their part in the celebrations, the Churches Together decided to hold a festival of faith during the month of July, culminating in a flower festival, a scratch performance of the *Messiah* and a huge outdoor service on the common. The festival planning began two years in advance, raising money, booking space at the civic centre for a photographic exhibition on the churches' work called 'Faith makes a Difference', and organizing a display on the history of the churches in the town in the large and historic parish church. There was also a pilgrim trail, around features of the town's Christian history, including the ruins of what was, until the Reformation, a flourishing monastery. In addition to the practical arrangements, a group of people met monthly to pray for the work of the churches in the festival. They raised questions about the emphasis on faith in history, rather than in the present and the future, and after discussion it was agreed that there should also be a children's holiday club run by the churches together at the Methodist church during July, and packs of supporting material on 'Faith in our Town', for use in schools. During the autumn there were also a series of Faith in our Town evenings, led by people from the community, sharing their experience as Christians in medicine, business, agriculture, education and the arts, and a programme of concerts in four of the churches. Another question was raised about how people of other faiths could be included, although their numbers in the town were very small; thinking about this question proved inconclusive.

The festival raised the profile of the churches in the town, and in working much more together they deepened their relationships with one another. During the festival year, the Churches Together group cancelled their usual programme of activities, and afterwards decided not to reinstate most of them, but to concentrate on working together in some particular areas where they could see a need, and to pool their resources. The Methodist and URC churches agreed to go on organizing the children's holiday club, on behalf of all the churches, and the Anglican daughter church has now become a focus for work with young people.

- How could churches in your area join in celebrating their common faith together?

IN RELATIONS WITH PEOPLE OF OTHER FAITHS

In a port city with a very diverse population, including a large and long-standing Jewish community and smaller groups of Muslim, Hindu and Sikh people, the Churches Together approached leaders of the other faith communities with the suggestion that an interfaith forum might be established. After several years of careful exploration, the forum had a cautious beginning, but has now become well established as a place for dialogue, organizing lectures, sharing information and friendship. When it became apparent that the faith communities would have to relate to new government regional structures through a single representative, the forum played an important role in enabling discussion across the region among communities who did not know one another so well.

- How could the churches in your area work to establish closer relations with other faith communities?

IN SOCIAL RESPONSIBILITY

In the West Midlands, after a review of their work in social responsibility, a diocese invited partner churches at the Intermediate level to share with them in a new body to work on behalf of all the churches. Five partner churches agreed to resource the work together, and the joint work now fulfils the role undertaken by the former denominational social responsibility committees. The churches employ a full-time officer to work on their behalf.

- In what ways could the churches in your area co-ordinate their work in social responsibility?

IN WORLD DEVELOPMENT

In a small town, the Churches Together have, for several years, made Christian Aid Week and One World Week a focus of their activities, going into schools, doing street theatre in the market place and selling fairly traded goods, among other things. The town was active in twinning with partner communities in France and Germany, and the Churches Together is also a part of these activities, with excellent relationships with churches in the twin towns. The One World group suggested that they might also form a partnership with a community outside Europe, and they have now established a link with a town in West Africa, where the diocese is a partner of the Church of England diocese. The link is based not on aid or sponsorship, but on friendship and learning about one another. The town has now also become part of this friendship link, and two teachers have visited schools in the link community, bringing back information and contacts for future work.

- How could the churches in your area participate in raising the profile of world development issues?

IN EDUCATION

In a seaside town, it was agreed to build a primary school to serve a new housing area. The Church of England and the Methodist Church had already agreed to build a joint church in the area, and the joint school and church have been built on the same site, with separate but interconnecting buildings, which can be used by both and by the wider community.

In a new town, a large comprehensive school was built as the focus of a group of community facilities, including shops, a pub, a doctor's surgery and a new church building, which is the home of an LEP, which brings together Anglicans, Baptists, Methodists and members of the URC. The church was anxious to find a way of being involved with the school, which had a strongly secular ethos. The minister at the LEP, who was a Baptist, took occasional assemblies at the school, but felt that this was not an effective way of reaching the students. A member of the congregation noticed that the students wandered around the shopping centre at lunch time, eating sweets and chips, and wondered whether the church might run a modest café. She suggested this, and the idea was warmly received at the church council. The new church was already the home of a lunch club, and had good kitchen facilities, but the venture began with just wholefood vegetarian sandwiches, cakes, and hot drinks. The new café sold out of food in ten minutes on the first day, and now feeds over 100 students and staff from the school every day, along with shoppers and other people who work on a nearby light industrial estate.

The café has provided not only food for students, but also an informal place where students and staff can mix, and a way for the local church to offer low-key but effective chaplaincy to the school. At the request of some of their customers, the church now provides a weekly fellowship lunch for Christian staff.

- In what ways do the churches in your area work with schools and their students?

IN AGRICULTURAL CHAPLAINCY

In one East Midlands county, the churches at the Intermediate level have formed a partnership with ten other agencies, including the Community Health Trust, MIND, and the National Farmers Union, to set up a project to support farmers, agricultural workers and farming families who are at high risk of stress and mental illness. The project trains people as rural links, who are able to help people in crisis to access existing sources of help and support. Some county Churches Together bodies now jointly fund a part-time chaplain to agriculture, or rural officers, and a number of Anglican deaneries and Methodist circuits in rural areas have worked together to provide better support to rural communities.

- How could the churches work together to support the farming community in your area?

IN RURAL AREAS

In a sparsely populated valley nine Anglican, three Methodist, one URC and a Roman Catholic church serve a dozen villages. There are five clergy and ministers, two of whom are also responsible for churches in other areas, and two Readers and three local preachers who work together in the valley and meet regularly for prayer and fellowship. Over a number of years a variety of joint work has grown up between the churches, which are now joined in a covenant partnership:

- The Readers and local preachers all lead worship in the Anglican, URC and Methodist churches.
- In those villages where there is only one church, that church has made a declaration of ecumenical welcome and commitment.
- The churches share a part-time youth worker, who liaises with

the statutory youth services and works across all the villages, enabling the churches to organize youth groups in two villages, which serve all the churches in the partnership.

- During Lent and Advent, the churches organize a series of quiet Saturdays at different locations around the valley.
- In the summer, there are jointly run holiday clubs in three of the villages.
- From September to June there are monthly united evening services, which the churches take it in turn to host.
- During the foot and mouth outbreak, there was a telephone prayer group, involving over forty people who each made and received one weekly call.
- When the Anglican diocese was looking at deanery plans for pastoral reorganization, the partnership made a submission, which contributed to the final agreed plan.

In the West Country, a county Churches Together has undertaken a project to map the churches' resources, in plant and personnel, in a number of the community areas. The information has proved valuable both for the county council and for the churches in their future planning. The county council was surprised at the level of resources that the churches committed to rural communities.

IN MARKET TOWNS

In a market town the Churches Together group decided, following an away day for the ecumenical council of clergy, ministers and lay people, that they would move towards becoming a covenant partnership, in which all the churches – the Anglicans, Methodists, URC, Quakers and Roman Catholics – would participate. They worked with the CEO to draw up a declaration of intent, which took account of their existing shared work, but which also set goals for future development. They also drew up a constitution, and the CEO helped them to work out a suitable structure, based on the CTE guidelines, to support their relationship without adding a greater burden of meetings. After considerable discussion, they agreed that there should be sharing agreements on the two Church of England buildings and on the URC and Methodist churches; among other things, this would enable the sharing of buildings for weddings, which would not otherwise be possible. These documents were discussed, amended and agreed by the appropriate denominational bodies.

The partnership was inaugurated at a service in the Anglican parish church, where the church leaders – both locally and from the county Churches Together that is now the sponsoring body – signed the covenant. The Anglican bishop preached on the theme of commitment to one another and to the town. Each year since, the partnership have marked the anniversary of the signing with a service in which they renew the covenant with one another, under God. This annual renewal has proved important, especially as clergy and ministers have moved on and been replaced. A monthly staff meeting brings together the Anglican team of team rector, team vicar and curate, the Methodist and URC ministers (who both also serve churches outside the partnership), the Roman Catholic parish priest (whose parish is much wider than the partnership area), and a Quaker representative. The partnership council, which includes lay representatives, meets four times a year; with many changes of clergy the role of lay people in maintaining continuity in relationships has been especially important.

The partnership has a joint monthly magazine, into which each of the churches puts an insert for their own congregation. They run a coffee drop-in for young parents, midweek services, work with children and young people, and a lunch club together and also undertake work together in baptism and confirmation preparation and with bereaved people. There are four prayer groups, which meet monthly to pray for different areas of the parish, and a group that meets monthly for silent reflection on a passage of Scripture, which is hosted jointly by a Quaker and a Roman Catholic. Some areas of work are co-ordinated by one or two churches on behalf of them all, and most of the life of the partnership is expressed in the way that the churches share their daily lives with one another.

- How could working together in your area move forward through setting up a covenant partnership?

IN INNER-CITY AREAS

In two inner-city areas, different models of working together have been developed:

In one area, five small churches – two Anglican, one Methodist, one URC and one Moravian – have grouped themselves together into a cluster, to share resources. As a fairly new covenant partnership, they are gradually developing joint work, and will eventually reorganize their five existing buildings, several of which are in a poor state, on to three sites, with two new multi-purpose buildings to serve both the churches and the communities. They are sharing worship, lay training, prayer groups and a magazine, and are looking at sharing two lunch clubs and two afternoon fellowship groups between them. The ministers meet every two weeks, and provide holiday and day-off cover for one another. A partnership council of ministers and lay people meets quarterly at present.

In the other inner-city area, the parishes inside the ring road have been identified as a churches action zone, in which the churches that are partners in the Intermediate body have committed themselves to suspend their working culture, in response to the needs of the area. The churches have put aside their existing boundaries, and are looking together at more flexible and responsive ways of being the Church, in an area with a high level of social exclusion and a complex multi-faith population.

- In what ways are the churches in your area responding to the particular needs of your locality?

IN NEW HOUSING AREAS

On the outskirts of a cathedral city in the West Midlands, an area of new private housing was begun in 1981. As the very first houses were built, the Church of England appointed a deaconess to work as an assistant in the parish, based at the historic village church, which would soon be surrounded by new buildings. She and her family lived in the new area, and she visited every house as it was finished and became occupied. As the estate grew, pressures on the existing village primary school and doctor's surgery became acute, and became the focus of resentment for people who lived in the village. As someone who was part of both communities, the deaconess was able to help to diffuse some of the tension, and she campaigned successfully, with community groups, for the early provision of school and health services for the new housing area. In the mid-1980s the churches agreed that they would build a new church on the estate, which would be a single congregation LEP bringing together Anglicans, Baptists, Methodists and the URC. The deaconess was appointed as the resident minister, to work on behalf of all the churches, supported by a Methodist local preacher and by ministers from the other churches based in neighbouring congregations.

After her ordination as a deacon in 1987, the original minister moved on, and there was a period of vacancy, during which some of the lay members of the new congregation, now worshipping in the community centre, became more active in leadership. The new minister, who was a Methodist, found that he had inherited an ambitious, jointly funded building project for a new church. This was completed in 1993, at the same time as a new phase of house building was begun, and provides additional community facilities, including space for a lunch club, for health visitors to hold a clinic and for a playgroup. The average age of the Sunday congregation reflects the population of the estate, with many families and small children. The largest congregation of the week, however, is on Wednesday morning for the service that precedes the toddler group. The church now has a URC minister, who has brought a different, more community-centred approach, after the long period of concentration on the building project. Ministers in neighbouring congregations are no longer so closely involved in the LEP, as they have become overstretched and as the sponsoring churches have found the confidence to allow others to work on their behalf. A retired Anglican priest, who worships each Sunday with the LEP, also presides sometimes at the Holy Communion, and leads quiet, more reflective services for a small Sunday evening congregation.

In the North-East, an area of social housing built in the 1970s is served by an LEP that brings together Anglicans, Methodists and the URC. The congregation first met in a room at the local pub, and as they outgrew that moved first to the new infant school and then to the church building. This was built largely with funds raised by the congregation, and many of them donated their skills to help with the actual construction of the building. By the early 1990s, the population of the estate were badly affected by the decline in industry in the area, and there were serious problems with drink and drugs, unemployment, crime and vandalism.

The churches responded by committing themselves to share in appointing a resident minister, rather than sharing responsibility for the LEP between ministers who already had heavy workloads in other areas, notably the Anglican team ministry on whom much of the burden had fallen. The Church of England provided housing, and a Methodist minister was appointed. This expressed the commitment of the churches to the area during a difficult period and was much appreciated. The minister has worked in close partnership with the school, helping to set up an after-school club, and welcomes all those who work on the estate, health visitors, social workers, the deputy head of the school, the community police, etc., to a sandwich lunch in her house, once a month. This has improved communication and alleviated some of the stress of working in a difficult area. The churches have recently secured funding for a detached youth worker, but the minister remains the only person who works on the estate who also lives there.

- How have the churches responded together to any new housing in your area?

IN SUBURBAN AREAS

In a town in the North-West, the Roman Catholic and Anglican parish churches were located at either end of the same street, each with very active congregations, lively programmes and full churches on Sundays. Both were members of the town-wide Churches Together. Relations between the two churches had been positive for many years, with joint Lent groups and a shared project, reaching out to single parents living in an area of multiple-occupied properties at one end of the parish. Relations between the clergy were also good, and when a new Roman Catholic parish priest was appointed he, discerning in his own congregation the need for a better understanding of the faith and for a more mission-orientated outlook, invited the Anglican parish to join them in running an *Alpha* course.

This first course, which was run entirely for members of the two congregations, proved very popular, and was soon followed by further courses, aimed at drawing in more people from the fringes of both churches, and from the local community. Apart from strengthening their understanding of the Christian faith, the *Alpha* course brought the two congregations together, and people got to know one another. Two joint house groups and a joint prayer group were set up, and another group began to discuss the possibility of running youth and children's work together. Other areas of joint concern proved to be the need for more effective follow-up of contacts with families bringing their children for baptism, and older people living alone in the parish.

Both churches, which were already thriving, experienced a renewal in learning together, and they have found a fresh approach to their role in the wider community through their joint work.

- Have any of the churches in your area shared in running an *Alpha* course ecumenically?

5

Is It Worth All the Effort?

TRINITY AND UNITY

Few people can find the energy to face the hard issues of Christian disunity unless they find our divisions offensive, and unless they also hold on to a vision of our unity as a place where the Holy Spirit is at work. What many people discover, as they work with partner churches, is that we are much more than the sum total of all our traditions and, for all that we may become frustrated with the structures and processes, and sometimes with the people, the Church is still God's work – shot through with grace – and in working for the Church's unity we are participating in God's work, and working for the healing of a broken and divided human community.

So how does our unity speak to the world about the God we proclaim together? Working for unity is essentially about relationships and community, and it is important to remember that most ecumenism is, and probably always will be, informal: about friendship and being colleagues and eating or doing practical tasks together. There is always a balance to be struck between the relational and the institutional, and in ecumenical working this is especially important, as the temptation is often to try to come up with a system for holding the churches together as they are, rather than allowing ourselves to be transformed by the Holy Spirit, at work in our relationships. One of the most significant gifts of the Orthodox Churches to the ecumenical conversation is their constant insistence on the Trinitarian character of the theology of the Church, which always draws us to the God of relationships, who is in relationship in the Trinity of Persons. When our Trinitarian theology is weak our theology of the Church can become dependent on systems rather than on relationships; in the Trinity we find our pattern for community in relationship, dynamic and joyful in diversity and in participation between the persons.

GROWING TOGETHER

REPENTANCE, RECONCILIATION AND RENEWAL

As churches move into relationship with one another, and begin to grow together, paradoxically their divisions become more painful and more offensive. In this context, churches often find that they want to express in a public and formal way, in worship, their repentance for past behaviour towards one another, and for their failure to attend to God's call to unity. Such occasions can be helpful in moving relationships forward, even when wrongs were long in the past; the healing of memories is as important as the healing of personal hurts. If the churches are to work together in reconciling the hurts of the world, then they also have to face the painful reality of their own participation in those hurts and divisions, and receive together the forgiveness that enables them to change and to grow together as God's instruments for reconciling broken human communities. This is also an acutely personal business. We are often preoccupied with changing structures when we should be concerned about changing ourselves, about turning to God and repenting in the face of all the evil that our divisions have done, and of our own part in that, whenever we fail to love diversity, and to know our need of those who are different.

> It is all God's work; he reconciled us to himself through Christ, and he gave us the ministry of reconciliation. I mean, God was in Christ reconciling the world to himself, not holding anyone's faults against them, but entrusting to us the message of reconciliation.
>
> (2 Corinthians 5.18–19)

To turn to God in repentance is also to turn to one another, and to attend to the Spirit's work in our relationship, and to turn to the world, in response to God's call to participate in the work of reconciliation.

As churches grow together, and are able to repent together of the past and receive the gifts of reconciliation, to sustain them in their ministry as agents of God's reconciling love, so they also often experience renewal together. Working together is so often shaped by our efforts to get the structures right that we do not always remember to live as if our relationship as churches is a place where the Holy Spirit is at work, transforming and renewing our lives as we grow together.

KENOSIS AND KOINONIA

Make your own the mind of Christ Jesus
Who, being in the form of God,
did not count equality with God
something to be grasped.

But he emptied himself,
Taking the form of a slave,
becoming as human beings are;
and being in every way like a human being,
he was humbler yet,
even to accepting death,
death on a cross.

(Philippians 2.6–8)

So what are the qualities that characterize this dynamic of repentance, reconciliation and renewal, which is so often apparent in working for unity? Being in a real relationship means an openness to being changed by the other. As well as being open to the Spirit and to being renewed together, such openness also means being vulnerable to rejection, to hurt and misunderstanding. Working for unity, not only for the unity of the Church but participating in God's work of healing the hurts in a broken and divided world, asks difficult things of both individuals and their churches. In Christ we find a pattern for our relationships with one another; we are asked to live generously with the things which matter to us, always being careful that we do not make idols out of our own traditions.

Every relationship or encounter that we have with others, however brief, has the capacity to change us. As it is between individuals, so it is between churches; as we work together and grow in our understanding of one another we are also changed – not necessarily to become more like one another, but often to a more profound understanding of ourselves and appreciation of our own tradition. Of course, ecumenism should be about being enriched, rather than being impoverished, but in the context of our growing together, as we come to know and understand one another well, we may also be able to see our own traditions in a fresh way, through sharing them with others. And in the context of our relationships with other churches, we may come to distinguish between those treasures that we have been called to safeguard through the years of division, and that baggage which has weighed us heavily, and which we may now

set down. A willingness to let go of things that have seemed important in the past, for the love of God and the unity into which he calls
us, is an essential part of growing together. This kind of willing,
clear-sighted risk-taking is always in the context of obedience – in
Christ's case obedience unto death – for the sake of what is to come.
In entering the process of growing together, we learn to recognize
and to reflect together on the things that prevent our unity.

- In your area, what are the things that prevent the churches from
  growing together?

This kenotic quality is essential to the nature of relationships within
the Church which God calls us to become together, in communion
(*koinonia*) with one another in and through God. *Kenosis* can be
expressed in many ways:

- in listening to one another, and attending to the work of the
  Spirit in other traditions, taking other traditions seriously.
  When we are in conflict with one another, it may be a part of the
  process of discerning our common calling, but only if we are
  able to hear one another, and the Spirit at work between us;
- in a willingness to be changed together, in relationship;
- in according respect to one another, as to Christ himself, most
  especially when differences make our relationships difficult;
- in praying for unity with authenticity and integrity: that God's
  will should be done in the churches' lives. If we pray this prayer,
  and willingly open ourselves to renewal together, then things
  that feel important to us may be challenged and changed;
- in a readiness to re-examine our own cherished traditions, in
  the light of the experience of working for unity. We often find
  our self-definition in those things that make us different from
  others, and being part of something can feel so important in the
  face of the multitude around us, that things which are especially characteristic of our tradition or our history can come to
  assume a disproportionate importance. It is always helpful to
  ask why certain things feel important;
- as this kind of love develops, fear is also cast out, and we are
  able to grow beyond our defensive positions towards the kind of
  Church that proclaims the gospel in its life as well as its words.

Such sacrifices may not be asked of us, but the possibility of this
kind of generous offering, and the willingness to count others first,
must be a part of the pattern of our relationship, in growing

together into that communion of love and fellowship (*koinonia*) which reflects something of God's own life, in Trinity. This is a vision of unity which is lively: life-giving, sustaining and energy-releasing. It is also profoundly kingdom-centred, concerned with welcoming the hungry to share the feast that is set on the table in God's just and peaceable household.

DWELLING IN GOD'S HOUSEHOLD

As I have said, the word 'ecumenism' has not had an altogether happy reputation, and is regarded by many people as referring to something that is a boring waste of time, to the extent that we have sometimes had to find another language to talk about working for unity. This is a pity, because in impoverishing the language we use, our conversation about the scope of unity is also impoverished. The word 'ecumenism' is rich in meaning, and grounded in the same Greek root that gives us 'economy' and 'economical', and that also indicates the whole created order, stewardship and the household. So among many ways of interpreting the word 'ecumenical' is an understanding that speaks of God's householding of the whole creation. In the passage from the letter to the Ephesians that was quoted in Chapter 1, the writer offers a picture of God's household, which is built on the foundations of the apostles and prophets; and with Christ as the cornerstone, we are built up in him, growing together into God's dwelling place, in the Spirit.

This is God's household, the Church, into which we grow together, and in which we live. In this household the table that is set is the table of God's generosity, and it is a table where there is a place for everyone, and where there is enough for everyone to eat and be satisfied. This table is set in a hungry and broken world, and the call to unity is a call to be God's ecumenical instruments for the feeding and healing of that world. And this work of co-operating with God in building and dwelling in God's household is much too important to be impeded by the dividedness of churches.

Exercise 5.1: Developing in Your Work Together

- Think about the relationships in your own life, with other individuals and with your church: how have you been changed, in those relationships?
- How has your understanding of the Christian faith been

changed by encountering and working with people from different traditions?

- Plan an away day or weekend with your ecumenical partners, based on the repentance, reconciliation, renewal stages of this process, and focus on the ways in which you have been changed in working for unity. You might find it helpful to look at some of these questions:
  - What kind of ideas did you have about your partner churches before you began to work together?
  - What kind of experiences did you bring from working with other Christians in different situations; for example, at work or in another place where you have lived?
  - How has your understanding of your own tradition changed through working for unity?
  - What gifts and insights are you grateful for in each other's traditions?
  - What do you think your churches have to repent about their previous or current behaviour to one another?
  - How have you felt the Holy Spirit to be at work in your relationship and in your work together?
  - How has the locality where your work is situated shaped your relationship?
  - How has your ministry, as churches or as individuals, benefited from your working together?
  - How do you see your work together developing in the future? How does this relate to any plans which individual churches might have?

Exercise 5.2: Planning your Day Together

In practical terms, you need to consider the following areas:

- Who should be there? How should you invite people to participate, and how will the participants share the fruits of the day with others from their church?
- Do you want to invite someone to facilitate your time away together? Your county ecumenical officer should be able to suggest an appropriate person.
- Plan the shape of your time together to include worship, some input, either from among yourselves or from an invited

speaker, work in groups and in plenary and time to relax, over lunch.

- It is helpful to spend time near the beginning of the day listening to the stories and concerns of the partner churches.
- A suitable location. This might be anything from a church hall to a retreat centre; although it is convenient to meet locally, it is sometimes important to be away from your own patch, and find a new perspective on your work. If you have a small budget, a neighbouring church might be willing to lend you their hall for the day, and perhaps help with making tea and coffee, so that you are all free to participate. (You can always 'repay' them when they want to have time together by lending your premises.) Make sure that you have disabled access, wherever you go, and think about whether you need to meet somewhere that has a loop system, and whether any written material should be available in a large print form. Make sure that you can rearrange the furniture to suit your needs, perhaps for work in small groups, in plenary and for worship, if you are not using a church or chapel.
- Equipment. Will you be using a flip chart, large sheets of paper for noting group discussions, video or audio resources, spare Bibles, worship materials?
- Do you need to organise a crèche ?
- Catering. This might be provided by your hosts, at a cost, but you can also opt for bring-your-own or bring-and-share.
- Transport and finance. Make sure that whatever you are planning is accessible to those for whom it is intended.

Before your time away, discuss how the results of your deliberations will be shared with others from your churches. This will vary from church to church, with differing structures for discussion and decision-making. Are you planning to make recommendations for changes in the way you work together, practical action or developing your partnership? It is important to have a good spread of those who represent each church involved in the planning, so that you can take different structures and theologies of the Church into account when you are thinking about possible outcomes.

Finally, send a brief report of your activities to the county Churches Together, so that they are kept abreast of your developing work together.

128 *Growing Together*
CONCLUSIONS

For many years, work for Christian unity has suffered from being seen as, at best, a harmless hobby for church people interested in that sort of thing and, at worst, a wicked watering down of essential truths which others have thought worth dying or killing for.

I hope that, at least in the English context, we have now begun to break through some of the ecumenical pain barrier that has divided us for so long, and that has prevented us from having real, mature, truthful relationships with one another. Like all institutions made up of human beings, churches have a profound instinct to preserve themselves, to maintain the status quo and to defend their distinctiveness against the difference of others. I suspect that this dynamic is largely instinctive, and therefore hard to change, even in one's own heart; but what we need is exactly a change of heart, a conversion to unity, a fresh understanding of why the dividedness of the Church is important, and of how we have been implicated in the dividedness of the human community.

Working for unity requires us to be open to one another, and therefore to be vulnerable. In looking at how the theological process of growing towards unity might work, I have explored self-emptying *kenosis* as the stage in our development that comes before communion, *koinonia*. And this is not a game with Greek words, or a playing around with the existing structures as if, if we could only get them right, all would be well. I say this as someone who is devoted to what is called 'Faith and Order theology', and who thinks that the nature of the Church is profoundly important in salvation history. But the unity of the Church will not be discovered simply by getting all our cleverest people together in a room and keeping them there until they have cracked the code of our brokenness. The poet R. S. Thomas writes in his poem 'Emerging':

> . . . We are beginning to see
> now it is matter is the scaffolding
> of spirit; that the poem emerges
> from morphemes and phonemes; that
> as form in sculpture is the prisoner
> of the hard rock, so in everyday life
> it is the plain facts and natural happenings
> that conceal God and reveal Him to us
> little by little under the mind's tooling.
>
> (Thomas, 1983)

Most of the time what we encounter in working for unity is the 'hard rock', the raw matter of relationships and communities within which God is at work, which is why working for unity is so important. Talking about it is never going to be enough. As we share in God's work of building and transforming human community, and grow together into the spiritual temple that God calls us to become, we discover unity. It is revealed to us in those 'plain facts and natural happenings'. And as we wash up in other people's church kitchens, worship and work for the kingdom with them and say our prayers together, we become the Church together. The Church is glimpsed in all our churches; in all our diversity we are God's gift to one another, and our traditions are a means of carrying the gospel to the world. Our traditions mediate the truths of salvation history through different cultures and to different temperaments; we need one another and, more than that, we need to understand what really divides us from one another, because that is also what divides us from God.

Working for unity will change us. It may not make us more like one another – it may give us a much more profound understanding of ourselves, but it will change us. Being in relationship always changes us, as individuals in our ordinary lives just as much as churches working together. We are transformed in our relationship with one another and in our relationship with God, and it is in this transformatory quality that our relationship bears fruit. We become God's agents for the transformation of human community into godly human community; we become the Church.

Which is why ecumenism is far too important to be left to ecumenists.

Appendix I

THE EVANGELICAL ALLIANCE BASIS OF FAITH

Evangelical Christians accept the revelation of the triune God given in the Scriptures of the Old and New Testaments and confess the historic faith of the gospel therein set forth.

They here assert doctrines that they regard as crucial to the understanding of the faith, and which should issue in mutual love, practical Christian service and evangelistic concern.

- The sovereignty and grace of God the Father, God the Son and God the Holy Spirit in creation, providence, revelation, redemption and final judgement.
- The divine inspiration of the Holy Scripture and its consequent entire trustworthiness and supreme authority in all matters of faith and conduct.
- The universal sinfulness and guilt of fallen man, making him subject to God's wrath and condemnation.
- The substitutionary sacrifice of the incarnate Son of God as the sole all-sufficient ground of redemption from the guilt and power of sin, and from its eternal consequences.
- The justification of the sinner solely by the grace of God through faith in Christ crucified and risen from the dead.
- The illuminating, regenerating, indwelling and sanctifying work of God the Holy Spirit.
- The priesthood of all believers, who form the universal Church, the Body of which Christ is the Head and which is committed by His command to the proclamation of the Gospel throughout the world.
- The expectation of the personal, visible return of the Lord Jesus Christ in power and glory.

Appendix 2

EVANGELICAL RELATIONSHIPS COMMITMENT

THE 1846 PRACTICAL RESOLUTIONS REVISED

Living out our faith does more to promote genuine Christianity than merely professing it. So we seek to promote good Christian practice as well as true Christian doctrine, not least by the manner in which we conduct our relationships with each other. The British Evangelical Council (BEC) and the Evangelical Alliance have over recent years jointly sponsored an Evangelical Leaders Forum, to facilitate personal contacts between evangelicals within and beyond both these bodies. The 1997 meeting of this Forum asked its Steering Group to provide an up-dated version of the eight general resolutions agreed at the 1846 Assembly which launched the Evangelical Alliance, to guide members in their relationships with each other and other Christians.

The outcome is an Evangelical Relationships Commitment, which seeks to apply the principles of the 150-year-old resolutions in our contemporary situation. It is intended to stand alongside our Basis of Faith, and to express how we should be treating each other. It should be seen as an integrated expression of the responsibilities we owe each other in the Body of Christ.

The Executive of the BEC and the Council of EAUK commend this Commitment to members as a reminder of our basic Christian duty towards fellow Christians, and in particular as a guideline when making comments in the media, in book reviews and in public ministry generally. We hope it will assist in building better relationships at every level and in a wider field.

AFFIRMATIONS

- We welcome as Christian brothers and sisters all who experience the grace of new birth, bringing them to that fear and knowledge of God, which is expressed in a life of obedience to His word.

- We recognise our Christian duty of trust and mutual encouragement to all who serve Christ as Lord, not least to those who conscientiously prefer not to be identified with the same churches, alliances or councils as ourselves.
- We respect the diversity of culture, experience and doctrinal understanding which God grants to His people and acknowledge that some difference over issues not essential to salvation may well remain until the end of time.

ACTIONS

- We urge all Christians to pray as Christ prayed that we may be one in the Father and the Son, and so by the Spirit to promote personal relationships of love, peace and fellowship within the Body of Christ, His universal church.
- We encourage all Christians earnestly to contend for biblical truth, since only as we are open to learn from others and yield fuller obedience to the truth will we be drawn closer to Christ and to each other.
- We call on each other, when speaking or writing of those issues of faith or practice which divide us, to acknowledge our own failings and the possibility that we ourselves may be mistaken, avoiding personal hostility and abuse, and speaking the truth in love and gentleness.
- We owe it to each other, in making public comment on the alleged statements of our fellow Christians, first to confer directly with them and to establish what was actually intended and then to commend what we can, to weigh the proportional significance of what we perceive to be in error and to put a charitable construction on what is doubtful, expressing all with courtesy, humility and graciousness.
- We rejoice in the spread of the gospel across the world and urge all Christians to commit themselves to this task, avoiding unnecessary competition and co-operating, wherever possible, in the completion of Christ's kingdom of peace, justice and holiness, to the glory of the one God, Father Son and Holy Spirit.

Useful Sources of Information

Action of Churches Together in Scotland *see* **CTBI**

Assemblies of God in Great Britain and Ireland *see* **Smaller Free Churches**

The Association of Inter-Church Families
Inter-Church House, 35–41 Lower Marsh, London SE1 7RL
E-mail: aife@msn.com

The Baptist Union of Great Britain
Baptist House, PO Box 44, 129 Broadway, Didcot, Oxfordshire
OX11 8RT
Tel: 01235 517700
Fax: 01235 517715
E-mail: baptistunion@baptist.org.uk
www.baptist.org.uk

Black majority churches
The *Directory of Black Majority Churches*, which gives national headquarters and local church addresses, is available from **CTBI**

The Church of England
Council for Christian Unity
Church House, Great Smith Street, London SW1P 3NZ
Tel: 020 7898 1000
www.cofe.anglican.org and www.cofe.anglican.org/ccu

Books: Avis, Paul, *The Anglican Understanding of the Church: An Introduction*, SPCK, 2000
Avis, Paul, *Church, State and Establishment*, SPCK, 2001
The Church of England Year Book, Church House Publishing

Churches Together in Britain and Ireland (CTBI)
Inter-Church House, 35–41 Lower Marsh, London SE1 7RL
Tel: 020 7523 2121
www.ctbi.org.uk

Action of Churches Together in Scotland (ACTS)
Scottish Churches House, Dunblane, Perthshire FK15 0AJ
Tel: 01786 823588
Fax: 01786 825844
E-mail: acts.ecum@dial.pipex.com

Churches Together in England (CTE)
27 Tavistock Square, London WC1H 9HH
Tel: 020 7529 8141
www.churches-together.org.uk and www.churches-together.net

Conference of European Churches
PO Box 2100, 150 Route de Ferney, CH-1211 Geneva 2, Switzerland
Tel: +41 22 791 61 11
Fax: +41 22 791 62 28
E-mail: reg@cec-kek.org

Cytun (Churches Together in Wales)
11 St Helen's Road, Swansea SA1 4AL
Tel: 01792 460876
Fax: 01792 469391
E-mail: gethin@cytun.freeserve.co.uk
www.cytun.freeserve.co.uk

The Irish Council of Churches
Inter-Church Centre, 48 Elmwood Avenue, Belfast BT9 6AZ
Tel: 028 9066 3145
Fax: 028 9038 1737
www.irishchurches.com

The World Council of Churches
150 Route de Ferney, CH-1211 Geneva 2, Switzerland
Tel +41 22 791 61 11
Fax: +41 22 791 03 61
E-mail: info@wcc-coe.org
www.wcc-coe.org

The Congregational Federation
The Congregational Centre, 4/8 Castle Gate, Nottingham
NG1 7AS
www.congregational.org.uk and www.unionchapel.org.uk

The Countess of Huntingdon's Connexion *see* **Smaller Free Churches**

The Evangelical Alliance
Whitefield House, 186 Kennington Park Road, London SE11 4BT
Tel: 020 7207 2100
Fax: 020 7207 2150
E-mail: info@eauk.org
Contact details for Evangelical Alliance staff, information about the
vision and work of the Alliance, and links to member organizations can
be found on the website at www.eauk.org

The Fellowship of Churches of Christ *see* **Smaller Free Churches**

The Free Church of England *see* **Smaller Free Churches**

Independent Methodist Resource Centre *see* **Smaller Free Churches**

The Irish Council of Churches *see* **CTBI**

The Lutheran Council of Great Britain
30 Thanet Street, London WC1H 9QH
Tel: 020 7554 2900
www.lutheran.org.uk includes a listing of places in the UK where
Lutheran services are conducted.

The Methodist Church
Methodist Church House, 25 Marylebone Road, London
NW1 5JR
Tel: 020 7486 5502
Fax: 020 7233 1295
E-mail: enquiries@methodistchurch.org.uk
www.methodist.org.uk

Methodist Publishing House
20 Ivatt Way, Peterborough, PE3 7PG
Tel: 01733 332202
Fax: 01733 331201
www.mph.org.uk

The Moravian Church in Great Britain and Ireland
Moravian Church House, 5 Muswell Hill, London N10 3TJ
Tel: 020 8883 3409 and 020 8883 1912
Fax: 020 8365 3371
E-mail: Moravianchurchhouse@btinternet.com
www.moravian.org.uk

Oriental Orthodox Churches
(Armenian, Coptic, Eritrean, Ethiopian, Syrian and Syro-Indian
Orthodox)
Aziz Nour, Secretary, Council of Oriental Orthodox Churches,
The Vicarage, Iverna Gardens, Kensington, London W8 6TP
Tel/Fax and voice mail: 020 8368 8447
E-mail: nour@antaccia.u-net.com

Book: *Such a Feast: Spiritual Nourishment and the Churches*,
       CTE Publications, 2001

The Orthodox Church
Fellowship of St Alban and St Sergius
E-mail:gensec@sobornost.org

The Religious Society of Friends (Quakers)
Friends House, Euston Road, London NW1 2BJ
Tel: 020 7663 1000
www.quaker.org.uk

Books: Gillman, Harvey, *A Light That is Shining*, QHS, 1988
         Gorman, George, *The Amazing Fact of Quaker Worship*,
         QHS, 1973

The Roman Catholic Church
Catholic Bishops' Conference of England and Wales,
39 Eccleston Square, London SW1V 1BX
Tel: 020 7630 8220
Fax: 020 7630 5166
www.catholic-ew.org.uk

Books: *Directory for the Application of Principles and Norms on
         Ecumenism*, Pontifical Society for the Promotion of
         Christian Unity/Catholic Truth Society, 1993
         Boulding, Sr Mary Cecily, OP, *Churches Together in the Parish*,
         Catholic Truth Society, 1995

The Salvation Army
United Kingdom Headquarters, 101 Newington Causeway, London
SE1 6BN
Tel: 020 7367 4500
Fax: 020 7367 4228
www.salvationarmy.org.uk

Smaller Free Churches

Assemblies of God in Great Britain and Ireland
16 Bridgford Road, West Bridgford, Nottingham NG2 6AF
Tel: 0115 981 1188
Fax: 0115 981 3377
info@aog.org.uk
www.aog.org.uk

Journal: *Joy* magazine

The Countess of Huntingdon's Connexion
General Secretary, Mrs Marjorie Crossley, 69 Jubilee Road,
Middleton, Manchester M24 2LT

The Fellowship of Churches of Christ
General Secretary, Mrs Hazel Wilson, 25 Robert Avenue, Erdington,
Birmingham B23 5RD

The Free Church of England
General Secretary, The Revd R. E. Talbot, 32 Bonny Wood Road,
Hassocks, West Sussex BN6 8HR
Tel: 01273 845092

Independent Methodist Resource Centre
Fleet Street, Pemberton, Wigan WN5 0DS
Tel: 01942 227768
E-mail: 106570.2444@compuserve.com

Wesleyan Reform Union
Church House, 123 Queen Street, Sheffield S1 2DU
Tel: 0114 272 1938

The United Reformed Church
Bookshop, 86 Tavistock Place, London WC1H 9RT
Tel: 020 7916 2020
www.urc.org.uk

Books: 'The Basis of Union' and 'The Structure of the United
         Reformed Church', sections A and B of *The Manual*, 2000
         (also on the website)
         Cornick, David, *Under God's Good Hand: A History of the
         Traditions Which Have Come Together in the United
         Reformed Church in the United Kingdom*, 1998
         Norwood, Donald, *One Church Catholic and Reformed*, 1999
         Thompson, David, *Where do We Come From?* 1996
         Thompson, David, *What Do We Believe?* 1996
         All the books listed here are published by the United Reformed
         Church.

References and Further Reading

Avis, Paul, *The Anglican Understanding of the Church: An Introduction*, SPCK, 2000.

Avis, Paul, *Church, State and Establishment*, SPCK, 2001.

Boulding, Sister Mary Cecily, OP, *Churches Together in the Parish*, Catholic Truth Society, 1995.

Butler, David, *Dying to be One: English Ecumenism, History, Theology and Future*, SCM Press, 1996.

Called to be One, CTE Publications, 1997.

Carpenter, Jenny, *Together Locally: A Handbook for Local Churches Seeking to Work Together*, CTE Publications, 1998.

Catechism of the Catholic Church, Catholic Truth Society, 1992.

The Church of England Year Book, Church House Publishing.

Cole, John, *How to be a Local Church* at www.ctal.org.uk

Cornick, David, *Under God's Good Hand: A History of the Traditions Which Have Come Together in the United Reformed Church in the United Kingdom*, United Reformed Church, 1998.

Directory for the Application of Principles and Norms on Ecumenism, Pontifical Society for the Promotion of Christian Unity/Catholic Truth Society, 1993.

Ecumenical Relations: Canons B43 and B44: Code of Practice, The General Synod of the Church of England, 1989.

Gillman, Harvey, *A Light That is Shining*, QHS, 1988.

Gorman, George, *The Amazing Fact of Quaker Worship*, QHS, 1973.

Guidelines for Reviewing Local Ecumenical Partnerships, CTE Group for Local Unity, 1999.

MacMorran, Kenneth M. and Briden, Timothy, *A Handbook for Church-wardens and Parochial Church Councillors*, Mowbray, 2001.

The Manual, United Reformed Church, 2000.

Norwood, Donald, *One Church Catholic and Reformed*, United Reformed Church, 1999.

Not Strangers but Pilgrims, British Council of Churches, 1985.

Nunn, Roger, *This Growing Unity: A Handbook on Ecumenical Development in the Counties, Large Cities and New Towns of England*, CTE Publications, 1995.

One Bread, One Body – Catholic Bishops' Conference of England and Wales, Ireland and Scotland, Catholic Truth Society, 1998.

Podmore, Colin (ed.), *Community – Unity – Communion: Essays in Honour of Mary Tanner*, Church House Publishing, 1998.

Sharers, Guests or Tenants? The Sharing of Church Buildings in the Multi-cultural City, CTE Publications, 1999.

Sharing Spiritual Treasures, CTE Publications, 1998.

Such a Feast: Spiritual Nourishment and the Churches, CTE Publications, 2001.

Thomas, R. S., 'Emerging', *Later Poems: 1972–82*, Macmillan, 1983.

Thomas, Stuart, *One Lord, One Faith: Ecumenical Services for the Christian Year*, Kevin Mayhew, 2000.

Thompson, David, *Where do We Come From?* United Reformed Church, 1996.

Thompson, David, *What do We Believe?* United Reformed Church, 1996.

Welch, Elizabeth and Flora Winfield, *Travelling Together: A Handbook on Local Ecumenical Partnerships*, CTE Publications, 1995.

What on Earth is the Church for? British Council of Churches, 1986.

Williams, R., paper given to Affirming Catholicism at St Alban's, Holborn, 9 June 1990.

Winfield, Flora, *Releasing Energy: How Methodists and Anglicans Can Grow Together*, Church House Publishing, 2000.

Index